WILD ABOUT LEARNING CENTERS

PBS
KIDS
SM

Wild About
LEARNING CENTERS

by the *Between the Lions*® Staff
Based on the Award-Winning PBS KIDS® Literacy Series

BETWEEN THE LIONS is produced by WGBH Boston, Sirius Thinking, Ltd., and Mississippi Public Broadcasting.

BETWEEN THE LIONS is funded in part by The Corporation for Public Broadcasting, a cooperative agreement from the U.S. Department of Education's Ready To Learn grant, and by the Barksdale Reading Institute.

Visit us on the Web at: pbskids.org/lions

Printed in China through Asia Pacific Offset, April 2011. This product conforms to CPSIA 2008.

Published by Gryphon House, Inc.
10770 Columbia Pike, Suite 201, Silver Spring, MD 20901
301.595.9500; 301.595.0051 (fax); 800.638.0928 (toll-free)

Visit us on the web at www.gryphonhouse.com

© Photographs by WGBH Educational Foundation and Sirius Thinking, Ltd. All rights reserved *or* by ©iStockphoto LP 2011. All rights reserved. www.istockphoto.com.

Library of Congress Cataloging-in-Publication Data

Wild about learning centers : literacy experiences for the preschool classroom / by the Between the lions staff.
   p. cm.
 ISBN 978-0-87659-353-0
1. Language arts (Preschool) 2. Classroom learning centers. I. Between the lions (Television program)
 LB1140.5.L3W54 2011
 372.6--dc22

                               2011003159

Table of Contents

Introduction

Between the Lions is an award-winning PBS children's television series featuring a family of lions—Theo, Cleo, Lionel, and Leona—who run a library like no other. The doors "between the lions" swing open to reveal a place in which characters pop off the pages of books, letters sing, and words come alive.

This book, *Wild About Learning Centers*, was written by the same people who created *Between the Lions*. You can use the activities and ideas in this book during learning center time to practice key literacy and other important readiness skills. *Wild About Learning Centers* is designed to help young children develop a strong foundation in early literacy. The activities follow a program scope and sequence (see pages 14–15), that is aligned with state preschool standards and national Head Start frameworks.

This introduction provides an overview of *Wild About Learning Centers*, the literacy scope and sequence used in the book, a checklist to help you set up your learning centers, as well as a glossary that explains the meaning of important literacy terms.

Overview of Wild About Learning Centers

Each of the twelve chapters in *Wild About Learning Centers* focuses on one theme, reflecting topics that are interesting to young children and that teachers usually cover each year. The following themes are featured in *Wild About Learning Centers:*

Adventures
Animals
Clothing
Colors
Families
Feelings
Food
Friends
Homes and Houses
Music
Nighttime
Plants

Look for Click the Mouse!
Click the Mouse is a character on the award-winning show *Between the Lions*. When she appears on the show, something remarkable happens! Click the Mouse and the website address of pbskids.org/lions/gryphonhouse appear on many pages of *Wild About Learning Centers* followed by a list of stories, poems, songs, video clips, and/or games that complement the activity on that page and enhance your work in the classroom. Share this website with the children's families so they can use the stories, songs, poems, video clips, and games to support what their children are learning in your classroom.

The Building Blocks of Literacy

It is essential that all children develop the following building blocks of literacy. Each component is described and then presented in chart form on pages 14–15.

Oral Language: Listening and Speaking

Research tells us that before children become readers, they need to listen and talk a lot. Keep your classroom alive with the sounds of children talking, singing, and playing with the sounds in words.

Have conversations with children about topics that interest them, introducing new words and concepts and inviting children to talk about their lives. Throughout the day, create opportunities for children to listen to environmental sounds, music, songs, poems, chants, and stories. Focused talk around listening activities builds children's listening and speaking vocabulary.

Book Appreciation and Knowledge

Love of books and the joys of reading are at the heart of a successful literacy program. Children enjoy many different kinds of books, including favorite folktales, rhyming books, alphabet books, and concept books. Include a variety of books in your classroom to spark children's interest in books.

Story Comprehension

A strong foundation in story comprehension in preschool will help children become good readers in elementary school. Build opportunities for children to make connections between stories and their lives; predict what will happen next in a story; and understand that stories have a beginning, middle, and end. Fun after-reading activities, such as storyboard retellings and character interviews, help the children deepen their understanding of a story.

Phonological and Phonemic Awareness

Words and their sounds are what children "play with" to build a solid foundation in phonological awareness. Use the activities in *Wild About Learning Centers* to help children learn to listen and rhyme, and to practice skills in sound discrimination, hearing word parts, and blending sounds.

Concepts of Print

The activities in *Wild About Learning Centers* help children learn that print conveys meaning and that there are many great reasons to read and to write. As they watch you read books, children notice that reading is done from top to bottom and from left to right. Song and poem charts, environmental print, and writing activities also help children learn about letters and words, the spaces between words, and the direction in which words are read on a page.

Alphabet Knowledge and Letter Recognition

Name games, word walls, word charts, and alphabet, song, and poem charts help children recognize letters in familiar words and associate the names of letters with their shapes and sounds. Tactile letter shaping, letter sorting, writing, art, and movement activities offer multiple ways for children to learn how to form letters.

Beginning Writing

Children are motivated to learn to write when they discover that what they think and say can be written down and read by others. Children learn to write by observing others write. Observing what you write on class charts shows children that charts can describe their experiences. Children can also respond to stories by drawing, scribbling, or dictating their stories, thoughts, and ideas.

The activities in *Wild About Learning Centers* provide information, ideas, and activities to help children become good readers and writers.

Reading Aloud

Reading books aloud is the foundation of early literacy. Researchers have concluded that reading aloud may be the most important thing we can do to prepare toddlers and preschoolers for learning how to read and to write. *How* you read, and *what* you talk about before and after reading are just as important as what you read. Consider the following when reading books to young children:

- **Read the book several times** to yourself before sharing it with children. Mark the places at which you would like to pause and ask questions or explain unfamiliar words.

- **Talk about the book cover.** Point to the title, author, and illustrator, and talk about what they do. Look at and talk about the art.
- **Create a context.** Share a related personal experience, look at the pictures together, or ask children to predict what might happen in the story.
- **Read slowly** so children can understand and enjoy the rhythm of the words and explore the pictures. Hold the book so everyone can see it.

- **Add drama** to your reading by using different voices and simple props. Don't be afraid to be silly or dramatic!
- **Invite children to join in** repeating lines and phrases such as, *I'll huff and I'll puff, and I'll blow your house in!*
- **Point to the illustrations** to clarify the meaning of unfamiliar words.
- **Use facial expressions, movements, and gestures** to demonstrate the meaning of action words.
- **Ask open-ended questions** after reading to help children think about, remember, and discuss the story. Encourage them to connect the story to their lives. Remember to pause for at least 10 seconds after asking a question to give the children time to think about their answers.

The Three R's of Preschool: Rhythm, Rhyme, and Repetition

Rhyming and singing are great fun. They are also wonderful ways for children to hear the rhythm and patterns of language and to play with words and practice their sounds—important steps to learning to read. Rhythm, rhyme, and repetition make words memorable. The songs and poems the children learn by heart today will help them learn to read the words in a book tomorrow.

- **Sing a song or recite a poem a few times** before inviting children to join in.

- **Add movements and gestures** to demonstrate the actions in a song or poem. Invite children to clap or sway to the rhythm.
- **Identify rhyming words.** As you sing a song or recite a poem, emphasize the rhyming words by chanting or singing them in a softer voice or louder voice.
- **Print the words to the song or poem** on a chart. You may want to add pictures for key words: *Twinkle, twinkle, little* ⭐.
- **Invite children to find familiar words and letters** on a song or poem chart.
- **Sing favorite songs** over and over again.

The Literacy Scope and Sequence

Although all children develop at their own rate and in their own way, every child needs to develop the following essential literacy skills:

Oral Language: Listening and Understanding	■ Listens to others with understanding ■ Listens attentively to stories, poems, and songs ■ Uses active listening and viewing ■ Recognizes environmental sounds ■ Listens to and follows directions ■ Develops varied and complex vocabulary ■ Listens to music ■ Listens to the sounds produced by musical instruments
Oral Language: Speaking and Communicating	■ Uses language to express actions ■ Identifies common objects and interprets pictures ■ Uses language for conversation and to communicate information, experiences, ideas, thoughts, feelings, opinions, needs, wants, and questions ■ Retells a familiar story ■ Uses language to recall a sequence of events ■ Develops and uses new vocabulary ■ Uses positional words in proper context ■ Speaks in simple sentences
Book Appreciation and Knowledge	■ Listens to and discusses stories (realistic and fantasy) ■ Listens to and discusses nonfiction and concept books ■ Learns how to handle, care for, and turn the pages of a book ■ Selects theme-related books to "read" alone or with other children ■ Draws pictures based on a story ■ Joins in the reading of familiar/predictable/pattern books ■ Seeks information from nonfiction texts
Story Comprehension	■ Understands the literal meaning of a story ■ Predicts an outcome and/or what will happen next in a story ■ Connects information from a story to life experiences ■ Differentiates reality from fantasy ■ Interprets illustrations ■ Develops awareness of cause and effect ■ Uses experiences to understand characters' feeling and motivations ■ Retells or acts out stories in dramatic play ■ Discusses story elements (character, setting, plot) ■ Compares and contrasts characters, settings, and events ■ Understands that stories have a beginning, middle, and end

Phonological and Phonemic Awareness	■ Listens to and identifies sounds in words (phonemes) ■ Listens to rhyming words ■ Recognizes rhyming words ■ Generates rhyming words ■ Understands that different words begin with the same sound (alliteration) ■ Distinguishes words in a sentence ■ Listens to and distinguishes syllables in words by clapping, stomping, or finger tapping ■ Listens to and begins to notice beginning sounds in words ■ Begins to notice ending sounds in words ■ Identifies initial sound in words ■ Segments, blends, and deletes syllables in compound words ■ Listens to and begins to blend beginning and ending sounds in words (onset and rime) ■ Listens to and begins to blend three- and four-phoneme words ■ Begins to become familiar with onomatopoeia (words that have a sound that imitates or suggests its meaning, such as *quack*, *hiss*, or *woof*)
Concepts of Print	■ Understands that a book has a title, author, and illustrator ■ Identifies the book author and illustrator ■ Locates the book title ■ Understands that English is read from left to right ■ Understands that English is read from top to bottom ■ Holds a book correctly (right side up) ■ Recognizes local environmental print ■ Understands that print conveys meaning ■ Recognizes the association between spoken and written words ■ Recognizes that letters are grouped to form words ■ Recognizes that words are separated by spaces ■ Recognizes familiar words ■ Understands the different functions of forms of print, such as signs, letters, lists, menus, and messages
Alphabet Knowledge and Letter Recognition	■ Begins to recognize letters ■ Recognizes his or her first name in print ■ Understands that the alphabet is made up of letters that each have a different name ■ Distinguishes letter shapes (straight line, curvy line, slanted line, and so on) ■ Associates names of letters with their shapes ■ Notices the beginning letters in familiar words ■ Identifies the first letters in words ■ Associates names of letters with their sounds
Beginning Writing	■ Experiments with a variety of writing tools and materials ■ Dictates stories or experiences ■ Represents stories, ideas, and experiences through scribbles, shapes, drawings ■ Writes for many purposes (signs, labels, stories, messages) ■ Attempts to write his or her name

Glossary

alliteration: repeating the same sound at the beginning of words, as in *Sally sells seashells by the seashore*

alphabet knowledge: being able to name and write the 26 letters of the alphabet

blending: putting together individual sounds to make words (*I'm thinking of a word that names an animal. It has these sounds: /p/ /i/ /g/. What's the word?*)

characters: the people or animals in a story

concepts of print: children's understanding of the different ways we use written language—as in letters, recipes, labels, and stories—as well as the way we write and read print. For example, printed words are separated by spaces; we read from left to right and from top to bottom.

environmental print: the written letters and words we see every day in our homes and neighborhoods that we recognize from the pictures, colors, and shapes that surround them. Examples include food and clothing labels, store logos, and road signs.

fiction: stories, essays, articles, and books that tell a made-up story, such as storybooks, fairy tales, and folktales

literacy: the skills and activities involved in speaking, listening, reading, and writing

making predictions: using information that you already know to guess what a story will be about or what will happen next

modeling: showing children how to do a task or skill before asking them to do it on their own

nonfiction: stories, essays, articles, and books that provide information or facts about a subject, including biographies and concept books (books about colors, shapes, sizes, and so on)

onset and rime: Onset is the initial consonant sound(s) in a syllable; rime is the part that contains the vowel and all that follows it. In the word *cat*, /c/ is the onset and /at/ is the rime. In the word *bat*, /b/ is the onset and /at/ is the rime.

open-ended questions: questions that can't be answered with a yes or no answer. For example: *What part of the story did you like best?*

phonemic awareness: the ability to hear and identify the individual sounds in *spoken* words. When the children hear the individual /m/, /o/, and /p/ sounds that make up the word *mop*, they are developing phonemic awareness. [In *Wild About Learning Centers*, the *letter* is written in quotation marks ("d"), while the *sound of the letter* is written between two slashes (/d/).]

phonics: the skill that matches *written* letters and words with the sounds they make. A child who looks at the printed word *dog* and sounds it out is using phonics. Children need a solid foundation in phonological awareness before they learn phonics.

phonological awareness: a broad range of listening skills—from being able to hear and recognize sounds in the environment to paying attention to and manipulating the individual sounds in words. Rhyming, singing, and clapping the syllables in words are examples of activities that build phonological awareness.

picture walk: turning the pages of a book from the beginning to end and asking children to look at and talk about the illustrations. Picture walks before reading help prepare children for listening. Picture walks after reading help children retell the story.

plot: what happens in the beginning, middle, and end of a story

print-rich environment: a classroom that displays words and letters that are meaningful to children in places where children can see and interact with them

retell: to tell a story in your own words and in the correct order or sequence

rhyme: the repetition of the ending sound of a word, as in Jack and *Jill* went up the *hill*

scaffolding: helping children learn a new skill step-by-step and gradually removing support as children become able to perform the skill on their own

segmenting: taking spoken words apart sound by sound. Clapping the parts or syllables in words and names is an example of segmenting (*A-bi-yo-yo*; *Ben-ja-min*; and so on).

setting: where and when a story takes place

shared reading: when a teacher reads aloud a Big Book or chart with large print and encourages children to read along on parts they can remember or guess

shared writing: when children dictate their stories or ideas for the teacher to write

spoken or oral language: the language we use to talk and listen

story structure: the way stories are organized into a beginning, a middle, and an end

syllable: a word part that contains a vowel sound. The word *dog* has one syllable. The word *an-i-mal* has three syllables.

vocabulary: knowing the meaning of the words we use when we speak, listen, read, and write

word play: playing with the beginning, middle, and ending sounds of words for fun and to learn how words work

Setting Up Learning Centers

Learning centers are areas in a classroom that offer child-centered opportunities for hands-on exploration. Each learning center activity in *Wild About Learning Centers* offers children choices that strengthen literacy skills and promote interest in other cognitive areas. The activities are presented in a meaningful context that enriches the learning experience. Learning centers:

- Engage children in learning
- Encourage development of the whole child
- Promote literacy
- Build independence and decision-making skills

Each topic in *Wild About Learning Centers* is supported by the following learning centers:

ABC Center
Art Center
Block Center
Library Center
Math and Science Center
Pretend and Play Center
Sand Table Center
Writing Center

The way you arrange your physical space greatly influences how children play, work, and learn. Following is a checklist to help you create a learning center environment that supports children as they expand their knowledge of language and the world of print and books.

ABC Center

- Is there an alphabet chart displayed at the children's eye level?
- Are there alphabet manipulatives (magnetic and plastic letters, letter blocks, sandpaper letters, letter stamps, and so on)?
- Is there a variety of writing tools (paper, pencils, markers, crayons, and so on)?
- Is there an ABC Center label with a picture?

Art Center

- Are art supplies and other materials labeled?
- Is there a variety of art tools (scissors, chalk, clay, yarn, paint, brushes, and so on)?
- Are smocks, easels, and drying racks available?

- Is there a variety of writing tools (paper, pencils, markers, crayons, and so on)?
- Is there an Art Center label with a picture?

Block Center

- Is there a variety of blocks and building supplies (wood blocks, cardboard blocks, connecting cubes, and so on)?
- Are storage containers labeled?
- Are toys, vehicles, people, and signs provided?
- Is there a variety of writing tools (paper, pencils, markers, crayons, and so on)?
- Is there a Block Center label with a picture?

Library Center

- Are books easy for children to see and reach?
- Is there a variety of fiction and nonfiction books?
- Are there books that reflect children's racial and ethnic backgrounds, as well as books for diverse cultures?
- Are book-browsing boxes rotated in and out of the center frequently?
- Is there a variety of writing tools (paper, pencils, markers, crayons, and so on)?
- Is there a Library Center label with a picture?

Math and Science Center

- Is there a variety of clearly labeled manipulatives for counting, sorting, making patterns, and so on?
- Are math and science tools rotated in and out of the center (scales, rulers, magnifying lenses, magnets, geometric shapes, and so on)?
- Is there a variety of both living and nonliving things (shells, rocks, plants, hermit crabs, and so on)?
- Is there a variety of writing and data collecting tools (paper, pencils, markers, crayons, and so on)?
- Is there a Math and Science Center label with a picture?

Pretend and Play Center

- Is there a CD or tape player? Are there different types of musical recordings and storytelling CDs and tape recordings for children to listen to?
- Is there a variety of dress-up clothes and costumes?
- Are manipulatives available for playing house, store, fire station, and so on?

Is there a variety of writing tools (paper, pencils, markers, crayons, and so on)?

Is there a Pretend and Play Center label with a picture?

Sand Table Center

Are there small objects that can be buried in the sand, including plastic letters and letter molds?

Are there clearly labeled shovels, rakes, buckets, measuring cups, scoops, and other sand tools?

Is there a variety of writing tools (paper, pencils, markers, crayons, and so on)?

Is there a Sand Table Center label with a picture?

Writing Center

Are topic-related posters and wall displays located where children can easily see and talk about the pictures and words?

Are mailboxes, envelopes, stamps, and other materials rotated in and out of the center?

Is the center filled with writing tools (paper, blank books, pencils, markers, crayons, letter stamps, and so on)?

Is there a Writing Center label with a picture?

Managing Learning Centers

The number of learning centers that you set up at any one time will vary greatly. Based on the age level of the children in your class, the skills and concepts introduced, and the amount of space you have for learning centers, you may have as few as three or as many as eight open to the children at any one time.

There are a few logistical things to consider when setting up learning centers in your classroom.

Are chairs and other furniture arranged so children can talk and play together?

Is the classroom space divided into small learning centers that are clearly separated from each other?

Does each learning center have its own storage spaces?

Are messy areas (Art Center) on tile floors or other easy-to-clean surfaces? Are they near water? Do loud areas (Block Center) have carpet or carpet squares to absorb the sound?

Are loud centers far from listening and reading areas (Library Center)?

Children need to have choices of activities in each learning center. Providing manipulatives and materials for free play is a critical element. Learning centers should also have activities that focus on learning specific new skills or building on previously learned ones. The activities in *Wild About Learning Centers* provide strong ties to literacy and the skills children need to learn and develop to become good readers and writers.

Introducing a New Learning Center Activity

Each time a new activity is added to a learning center, follow these steps to introduce it to the children:

Step 1: Model the activity by demonstrating how to do it step-by-step, thinking aloud so children can understand your thought process. Or, if it is an open-ended exploration, suggest a goal, problem to be solved, or big question to guide their play.

Step 2: Introduce new materials and tools, demonstrating how to use them.

Step 3: Introduce new vocabulary.

Step 4: Invite children to engage in the activity.

Step 5: Encourage children to complete the activity on their own or with another child.

Establishing Rules

Learning centers are intentionally active and fun. To ensure that the atmosphere in the classroom is pleasant and organized, establish rules for learning centers in the first few weeks of school. Display labeled pictures to instruct children about these rules. Review them frequently.

Establishing Routines

Set up routines and procedures that help you organize and manage the learning centers.

- Organize the materials, sorting them into covered bins, baskets, storage bags, and cans or on shelves. Label each container with both a word and a picture to clearly identify what belongs there. Be sure that each learning center has the materials needed for the activities you've introduced.
- Post a label that identifies each learning center (Block Center, Math and Science Center, and so on). Add a picture to support the word.
- Use nametags, colored clothespins, or necklaces to identify who should be in each center. For example, three red clothespins are

clipped to the Art Center label. When the children go to that center, they take one of the clothespins and clip it to their clothing. At a quick glance, the teacher knows that everyone with a red clothespin should be in the Art Center. Children recognize that when there are no more red clothespins on the label, the center is filled, and they will have to come back at a later time.

■ Set aside time for the children to clean up their center and display their work (when applicable).

The Teacher as Observer

Encourage children to work on their own or with one or two others in the learning center. As children work and play, observe the learning that's taking place. Stop to offer praise, answer questions, have children dictate responses to writing, use the new vocabulary, engage children in conversations, and suggest ways to challenge children or extend the activity. This is also a wonderful time to assess children's skills and to scaffold learning to meet the needs of all the children.

Learning Center Activities

Depending on the children's interests, you may want to modify existing centers and add new centers. When appropriate, demonstrate and model the activities. Invite children to explore materials in the centers and the activities on their own and in small groups. Encourage them to interact with one another and collaborate in their play. Provide assistance as needed. As you talk to the children about what they are doing, use the suggested vocabulary words in ways that help the children understand their meaning.

The chapters in *Wild About Learning Centers* are grouped alphabetically by topic and then by center type within each topic. Each learning center activity has the following components:

Age	Materials
Skill Focus	Preparation (if necessary)
Theme Connection(s)	What to Do
Vocabulary	

Age—the age (3+ or 4+) for which the activity will be most appropriate.

Skill Focus—lists the literacy skills that the activity addresses and other skills that young children need to learn, such as fine motor skills or emotional awareness.

Theme Connection(s)—lists one or two familiar early childhood themes that the activity covers.

Vocabulary—lists words that are part of the activity. Use these when you are engaging children in the activity, defining their meaning if necessary. Repeat these words throughout the day so children hear the words in context and can begin to understand how each word is used.

Materials—an alphabetical list of the materials you will need to do the activity. Be sure you have the materials you need before you begin the activity.

Preparation—If the activity needs any preparation, such as writing a song or poem on chart paper or preparing a chart, what you need to do is described in this section.

What to Do—Step by step, this section outlines how to engage children in the activity.

In addition, some activities include Extension Ideas that build on the main activity or extend it to another curriculum area.

Adventures

10–9–8–7–6–5–4–3–2–1–BLAST OFF! into an adventure in outer space, to find buried treasure or meet not-so-ferocious lions in the wild! The children in your classroom will have fun hearing about amazing adventures. They will learn about surprising places to visit and things to do while exploring the joys of writing, speaking, storytelling, and reading with friends.

An Adventure

Ride a bike, plane, or car.
Take a rocket to a star.
Hunt a lion, sail the sea,
An adventure for you and me.
Let's go!

ABC CENTER

Letter Hunt

Skill Focus
Fine Motor Skills
Letter Formation
Letter Recognition

Theme Connections
Adventures
The Alphabet
Shapes

Vocabulary
clay	roll
curvy line	search
find	trace
hunt	uppercase
lowercase	

Materials
alphabet card
blank index cards
glue
lengths of yarn
marker
modeling clay
pipe cleaners

Preparation
• Write the uppercase and lowercase "Cc" on index cards to create letter "Cc" cards.

What to Do

❋ Select one letter of the alphabet. Focus on a letter that relates to a classroom topic, a book you are reading to the children, or something that is happening in the classroom. In this case, the letter "Cc" is the example.

❋ Display the letter "Cc" card. Talk about the shape of the letter as you trace it with your finger. Point out that the uppercase and lowercase "Cc" look the same, except one is bigger.

❋ Encourage the children in the center to take turns hiding a few letter "Cc" cards throughout the classroom, and then another child or children can go on a Letter Hunt, pretending to be explorers in the jungle searching high and low for hidden "Cc" letters.

Extension Idea

Let the children glue yarn over the shapes of the letters on their "Cc" cards, or encourage the children to shape pipe cleaners or "snakes" of clay into the shape of the letter "Cc."

Click on the *Between the Lions* website!
pbskids.org/lions/gryphonhouse

Story: City Mouse and Country Mouse
Songs: City Country Rap | The Two Sounds Made by c
Games: Theo's Puzzles (c) | Sky Riding

Skill Focus

Compare and Contrast
Letter Recognition
Vocabulary

Theme Connections

Adventures
The Alphabet
Opposites / Shapes

ABC CENTER

Fish for Letters

AGE 3+

Preparation

- Make a fishing pole by attaching heavy string to the end of a yardstick or dowel rod. Tie a magnet to the other end of the string.
- Place magnetic uppercase letters with all straight lines (such as E, H, I, K, T, V, Z) and uppercase letters made with all curvy lines (C, O, S, U) in a plastic tub (the "pond").
- Cut out two fish-shaped pieces of paper. Draw curvy lines on one fish and straight lines on the other fish.

What to Do

- Hold up the letter "L." Trace the letter to show how "L" is formed. Point out that the letter "L" is made up of two straight lines.
- Hold up the letter "O." Trace the letter to show how "O" is formed. Point out that this letter is made with a curved line.
- Explain that letters can be sorted by their shapes. Show the children how they can fish for letters. If they catch one with straight lines, they should put it on the fish with straight lines. If they catch one with curvy lines, they should put it on the fish with curvy lines.
- Encourage the children to trace the shape of each letter they pull from the "pond" and think about whether it is made with straight or curvy lines before placing it on a fish.
- Model the activity by fishing for a letter. Say, *Look, it's the letter "E."* Trace the letter slowly. *It has four straight lines. I am going to put it on the fish with the straight lines.*
- Remind the children to put all their letters back in the pond when they are done with the activity.

Vocabulary

curvy	magnet
fish	pond
fishing pole	shape
letter	sort
line	straight

Materials

heavy string
magnet
magnetic letters
markers
paper
scissors
tape
yardstick or dowel

Click on the *Between the Lions* website!
pbskids.org/lions/gryphonhouse

Story: The Big Fish
Games: ABCD Watermelon
Sky Riding

ART CENTER

Lion Masks

Skill Focus
Fine Motor Skills
Imaginative Play
Vocabulary

Theme Connections
Adventures
Animals
Imagination

Vocabulary

cave	mouth
ears	nose
eyes	pretend
imaginary	safety
lion	scamper
mane	vine
mask	whiskers

Materials

crayons
glue
hole punch
markers
paper
paper plates
paint
scissors
strips of yellow, orange, brown
   paper
toy lions
yarn

Preparation
- Before the children arrive, hide toy lions in the classroom.
- Cut two large eyeholes into paper plates (make one for each child), spacing the holes so the children can easily see out of them.
- Punch a hole on the left and right side of each paper plate.
- Create an extra plate that you can use to demonstrate how to make a lion mask.

What to Do

✳ Invite the children to go on a "lion hunt" in the classroom.

✳ After the children have found all the lions, ask them to name the different features of a lion's face, including the eyes, nose, mouth, ears, mane, and whiskers.

✳ Show them how they can make a lion mask at the learning center using a paper plate. First, color around the eyes and draw a nose and mouth for the lion. Show the children different ways to make the mane. They can draw wavy lines around the face with crayons or markers. They can also glue pieces of yarn or rolled-up strips of paper to frame the lion's face.

✳ Help the children tie yarn through the holes on each side of their plates and fit the masks to their heads.

✳ After children have made their masks, they can wear them as they draw pictures of where lions live.

Click on the *Between the Lions* website!
pbskids.org/lions/gryphonhouse
Story: The Lion and the Mouse
Game: Fuzzy Lion Ears

Skill Focus

Creative Expression

Fine Motor Skills

Shape Recognition

Theme Connections

Adventures

Imagination

Space

Rockets on the Moon

AGE 4+

Preparation

- Read a great space adventure book aloud to the children. You might choose *I Want to Be an Astronaut* by Byron Barton or another book from the list on page 225. Adapt the activity below to go along with the book you shared.

What to Do

✳ Show the children the page in *I Want to Be an Astronaut* on which the astronauts take a moon walk. Let the children pantomime astronauts walking in bulky spacesuits to collect moon rocks.

✳ Invite the children to roll, pinch, knead, and pound modeling clay to shape moon rocks.

✳ Encourage the children to mold the clay into other space-related objects, such as an astronaut, a rocket, stars, or the moon.

✳ If appropriate, help the children expand the experience by talking with them about what they are creating with the clay.

Extension Idea

The children can use their clay rockets and moon rocks when they make a moonscape at the Sand Table (see page 37).

Vocabulary

astronaut	round
circle	shape
coil	space
moon	spaceship
moon rocks	spacesuit
outer space	triangle
rectangle	window
rocket	

Materials

modeling clay

plastic knife

I Want to Be an Astronaut by Byron Barton or other fiction or nonfiction books about space travel (See page 225 for suggestions.)

Click on the *Between the Lions* website!

pbskids.org/lions/gryphonhouse

Song: Rocket-Doodle-Doo

BLOCK CENTER

Airplane Trip

Skill Focus
Beginning Writing

Hand-Eye Coordination

Imaginative Play

Theme Connections
Adventures

Transportation

Vocabulary

airplane	nose
body	passenger
clouds	pilot
cockpit	tail
control panel	trees
imagine	wing

Materials

blocks

cardboard box

construction paper

markers

Preparation
- Make a control panel for the cockpit of an airplane. Draw or tape paper cutouts to a cardboard box to simulate a control panel. Include knobs, dials, buttons, gauges, a compass, and a steering wheel.

What to Do

✳ Put the control panel in the block area, and invite the children to create their own airplane out of blocks.

✳ Have the children use large blocks to build the airplane. Encourage them to lay blocks on the floor to make an outline of the plane.

✳ If necessary, expand the children's thinking by asking, *Where is the plane's nose? Where are the wings? The body? The tail?*

✳ Invite the children to imagine taking a high-flying adventure over the housetops and trees and into the clouds to visit faraway places!

✳ Suggest that the children pay close attention to the place where the pilot sits (cockpit) and what the controls might do.

✳ Have the children add seats for the "pilots" and "passengers." Encourage passengers and pilots to board the plane and use it for imaginative play.

Extension Idea

Post chart paper in the Block Center for the children to draw or write about their adventures on the airplane.

Skill Focus

Book Care and Handling

Choosing Books

Concepts of Print

Theme Connections

Adventures

Transportation

Book-Browsing Boxes

AGE 3+

Preparation

- Set up book-browsing boxes with many different kinds of books about adventures. Include both fiction and nonfiction titles.
- Create a written label for each book-browsing box.
- Draw a picture (or cut out a picture from a magazine) that relates to each book-browsing topic and put the picture next to the written label, so the children know the kind of books in each box.
- For this theme, you might have book-browsing boxes for cars, boats, planes, rockets, trains, hot air balloons, and bikes.

Vocabulary

author	pictures
cover	read
fiction	return
illustration	select
label	title
nonfiction	

Materials

fiction and nonfiction books about adventures (See page 217 for suggestions.)

magazines

markers

paper

scissors

tape or glue

What to Do

* Explain to the children that the pictures on the labels of the book-browsing boxes will help them select the kind of book they want to read and will also help them put the book away.

* Ask, *If you want to read about an adventure on the deep blue sea, which box would you look in?* (The box decorated with the boat.) *When you have finished a book about rockets, such as* I Want to Be an Astronaut, *where will you put it?* (In the box decorated with a rocket.)

* Encourage the children to select books that interest them and to look at the words and illustrations on their own or with a friend.

* Model how to look at a book cover to predict what the book will be about and then turning the pages to "read" it.

Click on the *Between the Lions* website!
pbskids.org/lions/gryphonhouse

Song: At the Library

AGE 3+

I Love Books

Skill Focus
Book Care and Handling
Choosing Books
Concepts of Print

Theme Connections
Adventures
Our World
Transportation

Vocabulary

author	illustration
care for	predict
cover	title
handle	

Materials

nonfiction books about transportation (See page 226 for suggestions.) and interesting people and places in the community (See page 220 for suggestions.)

Preparation

• Fill the Library Center with nonfiction books about transportation and interesting people and places in their communities.

What to Do

✳ Encourage the children to select books that interest them and to look at the words and the pictures on their own or with another child.

✳ Model how to look at the illustrations on a book cover, predict what the book will be about, and decide whether you want to read it. Say, *This book has a picture of a fire engine on the cover. A firefighter is using a hose to put out the fire. Isn't your mother a firefighter? You might like to read this book.*

✳ Demonstrate how to hold, handle, and care for a book.

✳ Show the children where to begin reading and how to turn the pages. Read parts of the book aloud. Pause to discuss the factual information in the book.

Extension Idea

If the children are unsure of the meaning of some words, use the illustrations to help them understand the meaning of these words. If the children are looking at books about firefighters, you might need to help them understand the meaning of the words *helmet, suspenders, boots, fire engine, tank, hose, ladder, tank, axe,* and *hook.*

Click on the *Between the Lions* website!
pbskids.org/lions/gryphonhouse

Story: What Do Wheels Do All Day?
Poem: Things to Do If You Are a Subway
Video Clip: Transportation

Skill Focus

Counting

Listen with Understanding

Number Recognition

Theme Connections

Adventures

Counting

Space

Countdown

AGE 3+

Preparation

- Decorate the learning center with pictures and posters of outer space.
- Write the numbers 1 to 5 on individual index cards.
- Write *Blast off!* on an index card.
- Tape the number cards in reverse order, from 5 to 1, on a wall in the Math and Science Center. Tape the "Blast off!" card after the number 1 card.

What to Do

- Model for the children how to make rockets by covering paper towel rolls with aluminum foil.
- Provide the materials so each child can make his or her own rocket.
- Explain that when a rocket launches into outer space, the astronauts count down the number of seconds left to blast off.
- Suggest that the children look at the numbers on the wall and point to or touch the numbers as they practice the countdown. When they reach the end, they can exclaim "Blast off!" as they launch their rockets into the air.

Extension Idea

Extend the countdown to 10. Add the numbers 6 to 10 to the wall in the center. Point to the numbers as you model the extended countdown: 10, 9, 8, 7, 6, 5, 4, 3, 2, 1, BLAST OFF!

Vocabulary

backward

blast off

countdown

numbers

outer space

rocket

Materials

aluminum foil

chart paper

fiction and nonfiction books about outer space and space travel (See suggestions on page 225.)

index cards

markers

paper towel roll

Click on the Between the Lions website!

pbskids.org/lions/gryphonhouse

Story: Deep in the Swamp

Song: Rocket-Doodle-Doo

Video Clip: Look at Me Fly

Mystery Shadows

AGE 4+

Skill Focus

Listening and Speaking

Observe and Describe Properties

Vocabulary

Theme Connections

Adventures

Animals

Opposites (Light and Dark)

Vocabulary

cave	flashlight
damp	guess
dark	shadow
explorer	

Materials

flashlight

shoebox

small plastic animals

tape

wax paper

Preparation

• Make a cave for this exploration. To do so, remove and discard the top from a shoebox. Cut out the bottom, so that only the four sides remain. Cover the top of the shoebox with wax paper and secure it with tape.

What to Do

✳ The children can pretend to be explorers looking into the shoebox "cave."

✳ Place the box cave on the table. Stand the box up on one of the wide sides with the wax paper facing out.

✳ One explorer puts a "mystery animal" inside the box and then shines a flashlight on the animal, casting a shadow on the wax paper. Another explorer looks at the shadow and tries to name the animal by looking at its shadow.

✳ The children can take turns selecting animals for the cave and guessing the identity of the animal by looking at its shadow.

Extension Idea

Ask, *What did you notice about the shadows? What are some ways you can make the shadows move and change?* Let the children experiment with shadows using the flashlight and the cave.

Skill Focus

Describe the Natural World

Imaginative Play

Interacting with Others

Listening and Speaking

Theme Connections

Adventures

Opposites (Open and Close)

Space

Into Outer Space

AGE 3+

Preparation

- Cut a door and round windows in an appliance box to make a "rocket."
- Hang paper stars, a moon, planets, and clouds in places where they will be visible from the windows of the rocket.

What to Do

✹ Encourage the children to be astronauts as they pretend and play together in this learning center. Maybe they will take a trip to the moon or explore new planets in outer space. Ask, *What do you want to take on your trip? Where will you go? What will you do? How will you get back to Earth?*

✹ The children can prepare a rocket for their journey by drawing or painting a control panel using red and green buttons, arrows, and gauges. Help them add labels to the control panel.

✹ Expand this experience by saying, *Mike painted buttons to open and close the hatch on the rocket. Let's write the words* open *and* close *on the buttons.* Continue with other labels.

Vocabulary

astronaut	explore
blast off	moon
control panel	outer space
countdown	planet
Earth	rocket

Materials

large appliance box

markers

paint and paintbrushes

scissors

Extension Idea

Learn an action poem about space travel.

Zoom, Zoom, Zoom
Zoom, zoom, zoom, (*Rub hands upward.*)
I'm going to the moon. (*Zoom hands up.*)
If you want to take a trip,
Climb aboard my rocket ship. (*Climb an imaginary ladder.*)
Zoom, zoom, zoom, (*Rub hands upward.*)
I'm going to the moon. (*Zoom hands up.*)

PRETEND AND PLAY CENTER
Obstacle Course

Skill Focus
Active Listening
Gross Motor Skills
Positional Words

Theme Connections
Adventures
Opposites (Over and Under,
   Around and Through)

Vocabulary

around   over
chant   through
obstacle   under
   course

Materials
blocks
cardboard boxes
toy astronauts or animals

What to Do

❋ Let the children make an obstacle course for toy astronauts or toy animals on the floor of the center by building a bridge and a tunnel with blocks, and placing small cardboard boxes around the floor.

❋ Provide ample time for the children to move the toys around the obstacle course that they have set up. Help the children name the positional words—over, under, around, and through.

❋ Say the rhyme, inserting "astronaut" or the names of the animal as the children move the toys through the obstacle course.

Over, Under, Around, and Through
Over, under, around, and through,
Look at what the (_____) can do!

The (_____) and (_____), go *over* it. (*One child makes the toys step over a box.*)
The (_____) and (_____), go *under* it. (*Another child makes the toys crawl under a block bridge.*)
The (_____) and (_____), go *around* it. (*The first child walks the toys around a box.*)
The (_____) and (_____), go *through* it. (*The second child places the toy inside the tunnel.*)

❋ Let the children create a new obstacle course with new objects for new toys.

Click on the *Between the Lions* website!
pbskids.org/lions/gryphonhouse

Story: Hide-and-Seek

Skill Focus
Fine Motor Skills
Imaginative Play

Theme Connections
Adventures
Imagination
Space

Moonscape

AGE 3+

Preparation
• Post pictures of the moon in the learning center. Include pictures of the moon from far away and from close-up with craters, mountains, volcanoes, and rocks showing.

What to Do

▣ Explain that a number of years ago, astronauts traveled to the moon in a rocket. It took three days for them to reach the moon. When they landed on the moon's surface, they got out and walked around. It is very different from Earth.

▣ Look closely at the pictures of the moon. Ask, *What do you notice about the moon? What color is it? Do you see buildings? Trees? Mountains? Rocks? Holes?* Explain that the holes on the moon are called *craters*. Point out that some parts of the moon are very rocky and have big mountains and that other parts are flat.

▣ Encourage the children to shape sand to resemble the surface of the moon. Model the process by piling damp sand into a tall mound. Say, *This looks like a mountain. How could I make a crater?* Encourage free exploration.

▣ Have the children use toy rockets and figures to simulate a moon landing and exploration.

Extension Idea

The children can draw a flag and attach it to a craft stick. They can plant the flag into the sand after the moon landing.

Vocabulary
astronaut	mountains
crater	rocket
flat	rocks
holes	surface
moon	volcano

Materials
markers
moist sand
paper
pictures of the moon
sand scoops and shovels
sandbox
tape
toy figures
toy rockets
wooden craft sticks

Buried Treasure

AGE 3+

Skill Focus
Gross Motor Skills
Interacting with Others
Speaking (Sharing Ideas)

Theme Connections
Adventures
Imagination

Vocabulary
buried   trinket
treasure   uncover
treasure
  hunter

Materials
sand
sand table
trinkets

Preparation
- Hide several "treasures" in the sand at the sand table. The treasures might be objects such as a strand of plastic beads, play coins, plastic spoons, toy cups, boats, scoops, and rings. Add trinkets that may be unfamiliar to the children, such as a compass, a sifter, and a seashell, to encourage discussion and speculation.

What to Do
- Have the children pretend that they are on a treasure hunt, looking for buried objects. Let them search through the sand to uncover the objects.
- Encourage the children to use their imaginations and create stories about the treasures that they found.
- Ask the children to bury the treasures again before the next treasure hunters arrive.

Click on the *Between the Lions* website!
pbskids.org/lions/gryphonhouse
Game: Monkey Match

Skill Focus

Concepts of Print

Listening and Speaking

Writing Name

Theme Connections

Adventures

Imagination

Transportation

Packing for a Trip

AGE 4+

Preparation

- Cut pieces of construction paper into shapes that resemble backpacks or suitcases. Provide one for each child.

What to Do

- ✱ Ask the children to think of an exciting place they would like to visit or a trip they would like to take. Ask, *Where would you like to go? What will you do there? What will you take with you?*
- ✱ The children can "pack" for the trip by drawing on the backpack or suitcase each item they will need.
- ✱ The children can write their name on their backpack or suitcase.
- ✱ Help the children label the items they "packed." Talk about the letters in each word. You might say, *Rosalita, I see that you packed a camera. You will be able to take lots of pictures of monkeys and lions at the zoo! Look at the word* camera. *It begins with the letter "Cc." You packed something else that begins with the letter "Cc." What is it?*

Extension Idea

Invite the children to talk about their imaginary trip and share their backpack or suitcase with another child in the learning center.

Vocabulary

backpack   suitcase

imaginary   travel

pack   trip

Materials

construction paper

crayons

markers

Roll an Adventure

Skill Focus
Dictating Sentences
Expressing Ideas
Word Recognition

Theme Connections
Adventures
Imagination
Transportation

AGE 4+

Vocabulary

adventure
airplane
bicycle
bus
cube
helicopter

horse
hot-air
  balloon
roller skates
sentence
train

Materials

construction paper
crayons
glue
pictures of transportation
  vehicles
small cardboard cube

Preparation

• Cover a small cardboard cube (box) with construction paper. Glue a picture on each side of the cube that shows a mode of transportation such as a bus, train, bicycle, airplane, and roller skates.

What to Do

✳ Show the cube to the children. Point out that each picture is a kind of transportation, which is something that helps you get from one place to another. Invite them to talk about the pictures. Ask, *What is the name of this kind of transportation? What do you know about it? What is it like to ride on a train? On roller skates?*

✳ At the learning center, demonstrate rolling the cube and naming the picture that shows on top. Model making up a simple adventure involving that form of transportation. For example: *This is a bicycle. I will ride the bicycle across the park to get to the playground.*

✳ Model how to write about your adventure. *I want to share my adventure with my friends. I will draw a picture of me riding the bicycle. I will draw the park and the playground too. Then I will write what happened: I rode on a bicycle to the playground.*

✳ Now, a child rolls the cube and names the picture that comes up. Encourage the child to make up an adventure with that form of transportation. Ask open-ended questions: *Where did you go? What did you do?* Encourage her to draw pictures and dictate the story of her adventure.

Click on the Between the Lions website!
pbskids.org/lions/gryphonhouse

Story: What Do Wheels Do All Day?
Poem: Things to Do If You Are a Subway
Video Clip: Transportation

Animals

Animals with snouts and trunks and beaks. Animals that fly and slither and slink. The world is filled with amazing creatures that do some pretty funny things. The children will come eye to eye with some of these creatures as they learn about the silly antics and fascinating features of animals.

Fiddle-I-Fee

I had a little cat, the cat loved me.
I fed my cat under yonder tree.
The cat went fiddle-i-fee.

I had a little hen, the hen loved me.
I fed my hen under yonder tree.
The hen went chimmey cluck, chimmey cluck.
Cat went fiddle-i-fee.

I had a little pig, the pig loved me.
I fed my pig under yonder tree.
The pig went oinky, oinky.
Hen went chimmey cluck, chimmey cluck.
Cat went fiddle-i-fee.

I had a little duck, the duck loved me.
I fed my duck under yonder tree.
The duck went quacky quack, quacky quack.
Pig went oinky, oinky.
Hen went chimmey cluck, chimmey cluck.
Cat went fiddle-i-fee.

AGE 3+

Letter Stripes

Skill Focus
Fine Motor Skills

Letter Formation

Letter Recognition

Theme Connections
The Alphabet

Animals

Shapes

Vocabulary

across

down

lowercase

straight line

stripe

top

trace

up

uppercase

Materials

blank index cards

crayons

drawing paper

linking cubes

markers

modeling clay

paper clips

pipe cleaners

tape

Preparation

- Write the uppercase and lowercase "Tt" on a large index card and on smaller index cards to create letter "Tt" cards.
- Tape the large card on the wall in the ABC Center.
- Place the smaller "Tt" cards in the ABC Center.

What to Do

✳ Focus on a letter that relates to an animal with stripes. In this case, the letter "Tt" is the example.

✳ Suggest that the children draw a large tiger and then draw straight lines to make stripes on its coat. Some of the stripes may go up and down. Some of the stripes, especially on the tiger's legs, may go across. If necessary, demonstrate how to make a straight line, starting at the top and going straight down or starting on the left and going across.

✳ Show the children how to trace over the lines on both the uppercase and lowercase letters to form the letters "T" and "t." Say, *The lines on the "T" and the "t" are straight like the lines on the tiger's coat.*

✳ Encourage the children to trace over the letters on the "Tt" cards and make the letters in the air.

✳ Repeat with other letters of the alphabet. Focus on letters that have straight lines such as "Ll", "Vv", and "Ww."

Extension Idea

Provide linking cubes, paper clips, or "snakes" of clay for the children to use to form the letter "Tt."

Click on the *Between the Lions* website!

pbskids.org/lions/gryphonhouse

Song: Library A to Z

Games: ABCD Watermelon

Theo's Puzzles (t)

Skill Focus
Compare and Contrast
Fine Motor Skills
Letter Recognition

Theme Connections
The Alphabet
Animals

Uppercase and Lowercase Letter Sort

AGE
3+

Preparation
• Use blank index cards and markers to make letter cards, one for each letter. Write both the uppercase and lowercase letters on each card.
• Place all of the magnetic uppercase letters in one bag or box and all of the magnetic lowercase letters in another bag or box.
Note: Depending on the age and abilities of the children in your class, you may want to limit the number of letters that you put in each bag or box.

Vocabulary
big	lowercase
curvy	match
letter	straight line
little	uppercase

Materials
blank index cards
cookie sheet
magnetic letters (multiple sets)
markers
two bags

What to Do
❋ Ask the children to select one letter card. (This activity uses the letter "Pp.")
❋ Say, *This card shows a big (uppercase) "P" and a little (lowercase) "p." In this bag, there are some uppercase, or big, letters. We're going to find all the uppercase "P" letters and put them on the left side of the cookie sheet. We'll put the other letters on the right side of the cookie sheet.*
❋ Model the sorting process for the children. As you take a letter out of the box, comment on the shapes. Say, *This letter has a straight line and a curvy line just like the big (uppercase) "P" on the "Pp" card. It's a "P." Let's put it on the left side of the cookie sheet. This letter has slanted lines. It doesn't look like "P." Where should we put it?*
❋ Let the children sort the remaining letters, encouraging them to identify the letters by name.
❋ When the children have sorted all the letters, they should put the letters back in the box for the next child or group.
❋ On another day, repeat the process, having the children search for "p" in the bag with the lowercase letters.

ART CENTER

Pig Noses

Skill Focus
Creative Expression
Fine Motor Skills
Vocabulary

Theme Connections
Animals
Colors
Parts of the Body

Vocabulary
animal   pig
nose   snout
nostril

Materials
black paper
crayons
elastic, string, or yarn
glue
hole punch
paintbrushes
pictures of pigs
pink tempera paint
white paper cups

Preparation
• In advance, punch holes on opposite sides of each cup near the rim. Tie string, yarn, or elastic to each hole.

What to Do

✳ Look at pictures of pigs. Tell the children that pig noses are called *snouts*. A snout sticks out from the animal's face.

✳ Suggest that the children make pig snouts. Give each child a plain, white paper cup. Let the children paint their cups pink.

✳ When the paint is dry, show the children how to add nostrils by cutting and pasting black circles or drawing large black circles on the bottom of the cup.

✳ Suggest that the children use the snouts in dramatic play. If the children need prompting, say, *Lionel and Leona, the lion cubs on* Between the Lions, *like to pretend to be pigs. They put on snouts to look like pigs. Would you like to do that too?*

✳ Invite the children to act out favorite animal stories such as "The Three Little Pigs."

Extension Idea
Other animals have snouts. Provide pictures of elephants, crocodiles, wolves, toucans, anteaters, seals, and dogs for the children to look at. Let the children use their creativity to make funny paper cup snouts for these animals.

Click on the *Between the Lions* website!
pbskids.org/lions/gryphonhouse
Story: Pigs in Hiding
Video Clip: Pig and Her House

Skill Focus

Concepts of Print (associate spoken and written words)
Creative Expression
Fine Motor Skills
Vocabulary

Theme Connections

Animals | Colors | Sounds

Old MacDonald's Farm

AGE 3+

Preparation

- Set out easels and smocks in the Art Center. Be sure to set the easels on a washable surface.
- Provide a rack, shelf, or other area for drying paintings.

What to Do

❋ Engage the children in a discussion about farm animals, showing them pictures of animals and having the children imitate the sound each animal makes.

❋ Sing the song "Old MacDonald Had a Farm" together.

Old MacDonald Had a Farm
Old MacDonald had a farm,
E-I-E-I-O.
And on that farm, he had some pigs (cows, ducks, horses),
E-I-E-I-O.
With an oink, oink here (Change sound to fit animal.)
And an oink, oink there,
Here an oink, there an oink,
Everywhere an oink, oink.
Old MacDonald had a farm,
E-I-E-I-O.

❋ Have the children use the materials in the Art Center to paint pictures of their favorite farm animals. Encourage them to mix paint colors to create shades that more closely resemble the animals.

❋ Extend the children's experience by asking, *What sound does your animal make?* Write the word (*moo*, *oink*, and so on) in pencil near the animal's mouth.

Vocabulary

animals	moo
cow	neigh
duck	oink
farm	pig
horse	quack

Materials

construction paper
easel
large paper
paint
paintbrushes
smocks

BLOCK CENTER

Block Farm

Skill Focus
Cooperate with Others
Hand-Eye Coordination
Vocabulary (Identifying Objects)

Theme Connections
Animals
Farms
Sounds

Vocabulary

animals	horse
barn	pasture
chicken	pig
chicken coop	pigsty
cow	sheep
farm	stable
farmhouse	

Materials
blocks
box or bag
fiction and nonfiction books
   about farms (See suggestions
   on page 221.)
pictures of farms and farm
   animals
toy farm animals or pictures of
   farm animals, blocks, and
   tape
writing materials

Preparation
- Post pictures of farms, farm animals, and farm equipment and buildings.
- Place picture books about farms and farm animals in the center.
- If you do not have toy farm animals, cut out small pictures of chicks, horses, cows, and other farm animals and tape them to blocks.
- Place the farm animals in a box or bag.

What to Do
✳ Let each child select an animal from a box of toy farm animals.
✳ Let the children use the blocks to build a farm, including places for the animals to go during the day and places for them to rest at night (barn, stable, pigsty, coop).
✳ Expand the activity by asking the children about the animals. *What is the name of the animal that you selected? What sound does it make? Tell me something about this animal.*
✳ You might model a response, saying, *This is a horse. A horse says neigh, neigh. Horses like to run in a pasture and eat grass and oats. At night, the farmer puts the horse in a stable to sleep.*

Extension Idea
Help the children make labels for the farm. Do they have a name for their farm? Help them write it on an index card. Encourage the children to draw or write additional labels to show which animals are in each section of the farm.

Click on the *Between the Lions* website!
pbskids.org/lions/gryphonhouse
Story: The Little Red Hen
Video Clip: Fred Says: rooster

Skill Focus
Compare and Contrast
Counting
Hand-Eye Coordination
Vocabulary

Theme Connections
Animals
Forest

BLOCK CENTER

Monkeys in a Tree

What to Do

✻ Ask the children to tell you what they know about animals that live in trees.

✻ Have the children build a forest with blocks. They can stack blocks to make trees for the monkeys, birds, bats, raccoons, squirrels, and other animals that make their homes in the trees. They can tape green leaves to the tops of the trees to give the animals shade and protection.

✻ Encourage the children to make trees that are different heights. If necessary, model this construction for the children. Stack blocks to make a tree as you say, *I'm going to make a short tree. It has only two blocks. Can you build a tree with three blocks?* When the child has finished, say, *One, two, three. Your tree has three blocks.* Compare the trees. *Your tree is taller than my tree.*

✻ Suggest that the children compare the heights of the trees. *Which tree has only one block? Which tree has the most blocks? How many blocks does it have? Which has the fewest? Which tree is tallest? Which trees are short? Which one is the shortest?*

Extension Idea

On another day, add a box of wild animals to the Block Center. Encourage the children to identify the animals by name and use the blocks to construct a habitat for them.

Vocabulary
fewer	short
fewest	shorter
forest	shortest
height	tall
most	taller
number words	tallest

Materials
blocks
green leaves or construction
    paper and scissors to draw
    and cut out leaves
tape
toy forest animals

Animal Book-Browsing Boxes

Skill Focus
Book Care and Handling
Choosing Books
Concepts of Print

Theme Connections
Animals
Habitats

AGE 3+

Vocabulary
cover   read
illustration   return
label   title
pictures

Materials
fiction and nonfiction books about animals (See page 218 for suggestions.)
magazines
markers
paper
scissors
tape or glue

Preparation
- Set up browsing boxes with many different kinds of books about animals. Include both fiction and nonfiction titles.
- Create a written label for each book-browsing box.
- Draw a picture (or cut out a picture from a magazine) that relates to each book-browsing topic, and put this next to the written label, so the children know the kind of books that are in each box. For example, you might have book-browsing boxes for forest, ocean, desert, farm, and zoo animals, and pets and bugs.

What to Do
✴ Encourage the children to select books that interest them and to look at the words and illustrations on their own or with a friend.
✴ Model how to look at a book cover to predict what the book will be about and then turning the pages to "read" it. Say, *I see a big bear climbing a tree. There is a little bear cub near the tree, too. I think the big bear is going to climb the tree to get honey for its cub. What do you think will happen? I want to read to find out.*
✴ Point to the first and last pages of the book as you model where to start and stop reading.
✴ Remind the children to put the books back into the correct browsing box when they have finished reading them.

Click on the *Between the Lions* website!
pbskids.org/lions/gryphonhouse
Stories: How to Be a Good Dog
            Sea Horse
Poems: Baby Chick

Skill Focus

Book Appreciation

Choosing Books

Concepts of Print

Theme Connections

Animals

Habitats

Sounds

Animal Books

AGE
3+

Preparation

- Fill the Library Center with fiction books about animals. Include books with repeated and predictable text.

Vocabulary

cover	predict
illustration	title
pattern	words

Materials

fiction books that have animals as part of the story, such as *The Enormous Potato* by Aubrey Davis

What to Do

✳ Read aloud a book with predictable text, such as *The Enormous Potato*. Invite the children to participate in the reading by making the animal noises.

✳ After the pattern of the story has been established, pause to let the children "read" the repeated words or to complete the predictable patterns. You might say, *The daughter grabbed the wife. The wife grabbed the farmer. The farmer grabbed the ___.* Pause to let the children look at the illustrations and complete the sentence.

✳ Say, *I wonder what will happen next.* Encourage the children to "read" the book to find out.

✳ Invite the children to select other books that interest them and to look at the words and the pictures on their own or with another child.

Extension Idea

Invite the children to imagine a different ending to the book or to make up their own story, using the pattern of a story such as *The Enormous Potato*.

Click on the *Between the Lions* website!

pbskids.org/lions/gryphonhouse

Story: The Little Red Hen

Video Clips: Cliff Hanger and the Giant Snail

Cliff Hanger and the Sneezing Zebu

Pigs in a Pen

Skill Focus
Compare and Contrast
Counting
Number Concepts

Theme Connections
Animals
Habitats
Numbers

Vocabulary
count
farm
fencepost
number words

order
pig
pigpen

Materials
craft sticks
glue
markers
number chart
pink paper
scissors
small milk cartons
small plastic pigs (or a set of pig
    counters)

Preparation
- Cut out 20 pink pigs.
- Label ten of the pigs with the numerals 1–5 (or 1–10).
- On another set of 10 pigs, label the pigs with 1–5 (or 1–10) dots.

What to Do
✳ Have the children match the numbered pigs to the pig with the corresponding number of dots.

✳ Encourage the children to refer to a number chart as they work.

Extension Idea
Suggest that the children use blocks to make 10 pigpens for the pigs. Put one of the numbered paper pigs in each pigpen. Challenge the children to put the pig with the correct number of dots in each pigpen. If you have a set of pig counters, let the children put the correct number of pig counters in each pigpen.

Click on the Between the Lions website!
pbskids.org/lions/gryphonhouse

Story: Pigs in Hiding

Skill Focus
Observing and Describing
Number Concepts
Sorting and Classifying

Theme Connections
Animals
Colors
Five Senses

MATH AND SCIENCE CENTER

Wooly Sheep

Preparation
- Collect a variety of woolen items, including wool before it's been made into yarn, wool scarves, wool socks, and wool yarn. Collect items with contrasting textures as well. Put all of the items into a box.
- Post pictures of sheep and lambs in the Math and Science Center. If possible, show a picture of a sheep being sheared.

Vocabulary
compare	same
different	sheep
feel	sort
fur	texture
lamb	wool

Materials
box
items with contrasting textures
pictures of sheep and lambs
two trays
woolen items (raw wool, wool
    scarves, socks, yarn)

What to Do

❋ Look together at the pictures of the sheep and lambs. Tell the children that a lamb is a baby sheep and that lambs have fur, called wool, that covers their bodies. The wool can be black, gray, or white. Let the children feel some wool.

❋ Sing together the song "Mary Had a Little Lamb." Replace the word "fleece" with "wool."

Mary Had a Little Lamb
Mary had a little lamb,
Little lamb, little lamb.
Mary had a little lamb.
Its wool was white as snow.

❋ Partners can work together in the learning center to touch each item in the box and describe how it feels.

❋ Let the children sort the items, putting the wool items onto one tray and the other items onto another tray.

Extension Idea

Ask questions to prompt the children to compare the textures of the items. You might say, *Does the scarf feel soft? Scratchy? Rough? Fluffy? Does it feel like wool? Then, let's put it onto the tray with the wool socks.*

AGE 3+

Act Out a Lion Story

Skill Focus
Comprehension
Imaginative Play
Listening and Speaking
Recall and Retell

Theme Connections
Animals
Forest

Vocabulary
act out
characters
events

story
story words

Materials
"The Lion and the Mouse" or another fable, story, or book about lions
story props
stuffed animals, puppets, or animal headbands

What to Do

❋ Recall favorite animal stories that you have read together. Choose one of the books to act out in the learning center. For example, you might choose the fable "The Lion and the Mouse."

❋ Hold up the book and read the title. Then turn the pages, pausing to look again at the illustrations to help the children remember the characters and the events in the story. Ask questions such as, *Who gets tangled in the net? What tiny animal sees the lion? What does the mouse do? What does the mouse say to the lion in the end?*

❋ Set the props in the learning center and encourage the children to use them to act out the story.

Extension Idea

The children may want to create new stories about the characters. As you visit the center, watch the play and provide positive feedback about the new storyline and their creativity.

Click on the *Between the Lions* website!
pbskids.org/lions/gryphonhouse
Story: The Lion and the Mouse
Game: Fuzzy Lion Ears

Skill Focus
Asking Questions
Imaginative Play
Listening and Speaking

Theme Connections
Animals
People in the Community

Roaring Good Tales

AGE 4+

Preparation
- Turn the center into a radio station. Hang a radio station sign (such as My Radio Station) in the center.
- Add a toy microphone and writing materials (clipboards, notepads, and pencils). If you do not have a toy microphone, make one from a cardboard tube and a ball of aluminum foil.

Vocabulary
answer   music
broadcast   news
interview   question
microphone   radio station

Materials
clipboards
markers
notepads
pencils
radio station sign
toy microphone

What to Do

✳ Talk about what happens at a radio station: people share current news, play music, and interview people. Say, *When you interview someone, you ask him or her questions.*

✳ Have the children take turns playing the roles of the interviewer and one of the animals they've learned about. One child might pretend to be the mouse in the story of "The Lion and the Mouse." The interviewer holds the microphone and asks the mouse questions. As the mouse answers, the interviewer makes notes about what was said.

✳ Model how to do an interview by asking the mouse questions such as, *What is your name? What happened to you in the forest? How did you feel when the lion set you free?*

Extension Idea
Brainstorm different storybook characters the children can interview, such as the rooster in *Cock a Doodle Moo!* by Bernard Most, or the cows and the ducks in *Click, Clack, Moo: Cows That Type* by Doreen Cronin.

Click on the *Between the Lions* website!
pbskids.org/lions/gryphonhouse

Story: The Lion and the Mouse

AGE 3+

Lion Homes

Skill Focus
Animal Habitats
Fine Motor Skills
Listening and Speaking

Theme Connections
Animals
Habitats

Vocabulary
cub   sand
lion   track
paw   wild
pride

Materials
glue
grass
green tissue paper
paper towel tubes
rakes
rocks
shovels
trowels

Preparation
- Make trees for the sand table by gluing "clouds" of green tissue paper to cardboard tubes.
- Provide clumps of real grass or small plants for the ground of the habitat. Or, use pieces of artificial grass or plastic aquarium grass.

What to Do

✳ Let the children create a place for a family (pride) of lions and cubs to live. Tell them that in the wild, lions often live in open areas with grass and trees.

✳ Set out a variety of props, including toy lions, rocks, grass, trees, rakes, shovels, and trowels. Let the children play with the lions as they work together to create a place where the animals can eat, play, sleep, and hunt.

Extension Idea

On another day, let the children make lion paw prints in the sand. Cut out a paw print from heavy cardboard and let them press it into the sand to resemble tracks left by the King of the Jungle.

Skill Focus

Listening and Speaking

Observe and Discuss the
   Natural World

Share Ideas

Theme Connections

Animals

Habitats

Dig, Worms, Dig!

AGE 3+

What to Do

✳ Sing this song about worms to the tune of "The Ants Go Marching."

The Worms Go Digging
The worms go digging side by side,
Stretch squeeze, stretch squeeze
The worms go digging side by side,
Stretch squeeze, stretch squeeze
The worms go digging side by side,
Making tunnels far and wide
As they all go digging
Deep under the ground
To get out of the sun
Dig! Dig! Dig!

✳ Talk about where worms live and how they dig and burrow in the dirt. Explain that the only feature on the worm's face is a mouth. The worm uses its mouth to eat soil and to push the dirt away to make a tunnel.

✳ Let the children play with plastic or rubber worms at the sand table. Have the children look for the worm's mouth. Encourage them to dig tunnels for the worms.

Vocabulary

burrow   sand
dig   tunnel
line   worm
passageways

Materials

plastic or rubber worms
sand
sand table

Click on the Between the Lions website!
pbskids.org/lions/gryphonhouse

Story: Wonderful Worms
Video Clip: Fred Says: wiggle

WRITING CENTER

Zoolicious Food

AGE 4+

Skill Focus
Beginning Writing
Concepts of Print (Functions of Print, Print Conveys Meaning)
Vocabulary

Theme Connections
Animals | Food | The Zoo

Vocabulary
banana
grocery store
meat

shopping list
turkey
zoo

Materials
crayons
glue
magazines
pencils
scissors
strips of paper

What to Do

✳ Have each child name a favorite zoo animal. Have the children pretend that the zoo animals are coming home with them! Ask, *What will you do with a zebra (monkey, camel, elephant, or other zoo animal)? What will you feed it?*

✳ Invite the children to make a list of food to buy at the grocery store and to talk about what the zoo animals eat and what they like to eat. If necessary to model the process, say, *I would love to have a lion come home with me. Lions like meat, so I will put* meat *on my shopping list.* Write the word and draw a picture of a kind of meat. Say, *I like to eat bananas and turkey. I will write* bananas *and* turkey *on my shopping list, too.* Write the words and draw pictures.

✳ Read aloud the completed list as you point to each word.

✳ The children can use a combination of scribbles, drawings, and pictures cut out of magazines to make their lists.

Extension Idea

On another day, have the children draw a picture to show what happens the day that the zoo animal comes home with them. Let them dictate a caption for the picture.

Click on the Between the Lions website!
pbskids.org/lions/gryphonhouse

Story: Owen and Mzee
Song: There's a Gorilla!

CHAPTER 3

Clothing

With this topic, the children in your classroom will learn about clothes—from everyday clothes to the special uniforms that people in the community wear. The children will sort buttons, make collages from old fabric, set up a tailor's shop, and design their own T-shirts. Who knew getting dressed could be so interesting?

I Can Do It Myself

Hat on head, just like this
Pull it down, you see.
I can put my hat on all by myself,
Without any help, just me.

One arm in, two arms in.
Buttons one, two, three.
I can put my jacket on all by myself,
Without any help, just me.

AGE 3+

ABC CENTER

Hunt for "Hh"

Skill Focus
Fine Motor Skills
Letter Formation
Letter Recognition

Theme Connections
The Alphabet
Clothing
Shapes

Vocabulary

clay	roll
curvy line	search
dot	straight line
find	trace
hunt	uppercase
lowercase	

Materials

alphabet card

blank large and small index cards

magnetic letters or alphabet blocks that include the letter "Hh"

marker

modeling clay

pipe cleaners

Preparation

• Write the uppercase and lowercase "Hh" on a large index card and on a few small index cards to create a large letter "Hh" card and small "Hh" index cards.

• Hide magnetic letters or letter blocks in the ABC Center and throughout the classroom.

What to Do

❋ Select one letter of the alphabet. Focus on a letter that relates to clothing, a book you are reading to the children, or something that is happening in the classroom. In this case, the letter "Hh" (for hat) is the example.

❋ Display the letter "Hh" card. Use your finger to trace over the curvy and straight lines on the uppercase letter and the curvy line and the dot on the lowercase letter to show the children how to form the letters.

❋ Let the children go on a Letter Hunt in the classroom, searching high and low for "Hh" letters in books, on posters, or elsewhere in the room.

❋ Ask the children to hide the magnetic letters or letter blocks in the ABC Center and throughout the classroom for the next group of children to use the ABC Center.

❋ Repeat with other letters of the alphabet. Focus on letters that are familiar to the children.

Click on the *Between the Lions* website!
pbskids.org/lions/gryphonhouse

Song: Hung Up on h
Games: ABCD Watermelon
Theo's Puzzles (h)

Skill Focus
Creative Expression
Fine Motor Skills
Letter Recognition
Vocabulary

Theme Connections
The Alphabet
Clothing | Colors | Shapes

ABC CENTER

Decorate Letter "Jj"

AGE 3+

Preparation
- Draw very large outlines of uppercase "J" and lowercase "j" on multiple sheets of paper.
- Cut out enough letters for each child to have one uppercase letter "J" and one lowercase letter "j."

What to Do
✳ Select one letter of the alphabet. Focus on a letter that relates to poems or stories you are reading about clothing. In this case, the letter "Jj" is used for jackets, jeans, and other pieces of clothing that begin with "Jj."

✳ Provide an uppercase "J" and lowercase "j" paper cutout for every child.

✳ Encourage the children to explore the shape of the letters by tracing the outlines of the letters with their fingers.

✳ Have the children use red markers and crayons to decorate the letters with polka dots, stripes, squiggles, zigzags, and curly and wiggly lines.

✳ Encourage them to talk about and describe the decorative marks they are making.

Extension Idea
Use masking tape to make an uppercase "J" and lowercase "j" on the floor. Encourage the children to jump (or walk, hop, or tiptoe) along the outlines of the letters.

Vocabulary
curly	red
dot	stripes
lines	wiggly
polka dots	zigzags

Materials
red crayons and markers
scissors
white paper

Click on the *Between the Lions* website!
pbskids.org/lions/gryphonhouse

Story: Joseph Had a Little Overcoat
Song: Upper and Lowercase
Video Clip: Monkey Cheer: jog

ART CENTER

Paper-Bag Vests

Skill Focus
Creative Expression
Fine Motor Skills
Vocabulary

Theme Connections
Clothing
Colors
Shapes

Vocabulary

arms
checked
flower
opening
pattern

plaid
polka dot
stripe
vest

Materials

crayons
large brown paper bags
paint
paintbrushes
markers
scissors

Preparation

- Make a paper bag vest for each child.
  - Lay a paper bag flat on a table with the open edge (top) toward you. Cut a line from the open edge up the center of the paper bag to the bottom. This will be the opening of the vest.
  - Cut a hole in the bottom of the bag. Be sure the hole is big enough to go around the child's neck.
  - Cut an armhole in each side of the bag.
  - Trim the front of the vest to create a V-shape from the midline cut to the cutout for the neck.

What to Do

* Point out patterns in the children's clothing. Look for examples of stripes, polka dots, plaids, checks, and flowers. Have the children with matching or similar patterns stand together.
* Distribute the paper vests. Have the children decorate their vests with paints, markers, or crayons. Encourage them to use different patterns and bright colors.

Extension Idea

Have a parade to display the finished vests.

Click on the *Between the Lions* website!
pbskids.org/lions/gryphonhouse

Story: Joseph Had a Little Overcoat

Skill Focus
Creative Expression
Fine Motor Skills
Vocabulary

Theme Connections
Clothing
Colors
Shapes

ART CENTER
Fabric Collage

AGE 4+

Preparation
- Cut fabric scraps into different shapes and sizes.
- Pour glue into shallow trays. Mix in enough water to make the glue thin enough to apply with a paintbrush.

What to Do

⚡ Have the children look at the fabric scraps and talk about the patterns. Help them with the words that describe patterns: *polka dots, stripes, plaids, checks,* and *flowers.*

⚡ Have the children make collages by choosing scraps of fabric and arranging them onto a piece of paper. Encourage them to overlap the fabric scraps on the paper. Continue until the entire paper is covered and each child is pleased with the arrangement.

⚡ Have the children glue the fabric scraps to the paper. If necessary, show the children how to press the fabric scraps firmly onto the paper to help them stick.

Vocabulary

arrange	pattern
check	plaid
collage	polka dot
fabric	scrap
material	stripe
overlap	

Materials
fabric scraps
glue
paintbrushes
paper
scissors
shallow foam trays

Extension Idea

Read the book *Joseph Had a Little Overcoat* by Simms Taback. Point out the patterns in the illustrations, such as the striped pants next to the black coat, the flowers on the dress, and the multicolored suspenders against the bright red shirt. Leave the book in the Art Center to inspire the young artists as they work.

Click on the *Between the Lions* website!
pbskids.org/lions/gryphonhouse

Story: Joseph Had a Little Overcoat
Song: Dance in Smarty Pants

AGE 3+

Junk Construction

Skill Focus
Creative Expression
Hand-Eye Coordination

Theme Connections
Clothing
The Environment
Recycling

Vocabulary

artworks	garbage
build	recycle
construct	structure
Earth	throw away

Materials

cans
cereal boxes
goggles
milk cartons
shoeboxes
plastic tubs
smocks
storage bin
wooden spools

Preparation

• Collect clean, used containers such as empty cans, cereal boxes, milk cartons, shoeboxes, plastic tubs, and wooden spools. Put them in a storage bin in the Block Center.

What to Do

* Explain to the children that we throw away a lot of garbage (or junk). One way that we can help clean up our planet Earth is to gather cans, boxes, plastic containers, and other objects that are going to be thrown away and use them again.

* Have the children dress like scientists, putting on smocks and goggles. Let young scientists sort through the storage bin in the Block Center, examining the objects that have been thrown away. Ask the children to think of ways that the objects could be used again.

* Invite the children to construct standing artwork with the recycled objects.

Skill Focus
Book Care and Handling
Choosing Books
Concepts of Print

Theme Connections
Clothing
Families
My Community

Book Handling

AGE
3+

Preparation

- Fill the Library Center with nonfiction books about community workers and the special clothing they wear.

What to Do

* Encourage the children to select books that interest them and to look at the words and the pictures on their own or with another child.

* Model how to look at the illustrations on a book cover, predict what the book will be about, and decide whether you want to read it. Say, *This book has a picture of a dancer on the cover. The dancer is turning and spinning. Isn't your mother a dancer? You might like to read this book.*

* Demonstrate how to hold, handle, and care for a book.

* Show the children where to begin reading and how to turn the pages. Read parts of the book aloud. Pause to discuss the factual information in the book.

* Let the children find the books they want to look at or read independently.

Extension Idea

If some of the words in the books are new to the children, help them learn how to use the illustrations and photographs in the books to understand the meaning of the words.

Vocabulary

author	illustration
care for	predict
cover	title
handle	

Materials

nonfiction books about community workers and the special clothing they wear (See suggestions on page 220.)

Click on the *Between the Lions* website!
pbskids.org/lions/gryphonhouse

Story: Night Shift
Song: Very Loud, Very Big, Very Metal

LIBRARY CENTER

Clothing Books

Skill Focus
Book Appreciation
Choosing Books
Concepts of Print

Theme Connections
Clothing
My Community

Vocabulary
cover
illustration
pattern
predict
title
words

Materials
Joseph Had a Little Overcoat by Simms Taback or other fiction books about clothes (See page 219 for suggestions.)
sticky notes

Preparation
• Fill the Library Center with fiction books about clothes and the people who wear them. Include books with repeated and predictable text.

What to Do

✳ Read aloud a book with predictable text, such as *Joseph Had a Little Overcoat.*

✳ After the pattern of the story has been established, invite the children to chime in on the repeated phrases or to complete predictable patterns.

✳ Point to the illustrations to help clarify the meaning of unfamiliar words, such as *overcoat, vest, scarf, necktie,* and *handkerchief.*

✳ Say, *I wonder what will happen next?* Encourage the children to "read" the book to find out.

✳ Invite the children to select other books that interest them and to look at the words and the pictures on their own or with another child.

✳ On another day, let the children put sticky notes on the pages with their favorite pieces of clothing. Sit with each child and ask him or her to share the choices with you.

Click on the Between the Lions website!
pbskids.org/lions/gryphonhouse
Stories: The Emperor's New Clothes
The Hungry Coat
Joseph Had a Little Overcoat

Skill Focus

Colors and Shapes

Sorting and Classifying

Working Together

Theme Connections

Clothing

Colors

Shapes

Button Sort

AGE 3+

What to Do

* Play a game of Pass the Button. Have the children in the Math and Science Center sit in a circle. Give each child a button. At the signal, have the children pass the buttons to the left. When you say, "Stop!" the children take turns describing the button they are holding. Ask questions about the buttons such as, *How many holes does your button have? What color is your button? Does anyone else have a round button? What do you think the button is made of?*

* Talk with the children about different ways to sort the buttons. Then model how to sort the buttons into the cups of an empty egg carton. For example, *I am going to sort the buttons by color. I will put all of the red buttons into this cup, all of the green buttons into this cup, and all of the yellow buttons into this cup.*

* Ask the children to decide how they would like to sort the buttons. Then, have the children look for the appropriate buttons and put them into the cups.

Vocabulary

button	shape
color words	size
holes	sort
metal	square
round	wood

Materials

empty egg cartons

variety of buttons

Extension Idea

Give each child a small pile of buttons. Have the children arrange the buttons in order from smallest to largest.

Click on the Between the Lions website!

pbskids.org/lions/gryphonhouse

Video Clip: un People: buttoned/unbuttoned

Game: The Messy Attic

MATH AND SCIENCE CENTER

Fabric Matching

Skill Focus
Color Identification

Matching

Sorting and Classifying

Theme Connections
Clothing

Colors

Shapes

Vocabulary

color words	polka dot
design	same
fabric	solid
pair	sort
pattern	square
plaid	stripes

Materials

clothesline

clothespins

fabric remnants

scissors

Preparation

- Collect fabric remnants from a local garment or sewing center. Cut each piece of fabric into two identical squares.
- String a clothesline across the Math and Science Center. Place several clothespins on the clothesline.

What to Do

- On a flat surface, mix and spread out six pairs of fabric squares. Help the children find the matching squares and hang them side by side on the clothesline.
- Invite the children to work on their own or with a partner to sort and hang other pairs of matching fabric squares.
- As the children sort, ask them about the different colors and patterns in the fabric pieces.
- Add new fabric squares each day.

Extension Idea

Sing a sorting song together. Sing the song to the tune of "If You're Happy and You Know It."

If Your Squares Have Stripes
If your squares have stripes, hang them up.
If your squares have stripes, hang them up.
If your squares have stripes
And you really want to show them
If your squares have stripes, hang them up.

Sing other verses replacing the word *stripes* with *flowers, plaids, dots, stars, zigzags,* and so on.

Tailor Shop

AGE 3+

Skill Focus
Creative Expression
Dramatic Play
Speaking and Communicating

Theme Connections
Clothing
My Community

Preparation
- Add items to the Pretend and Play Center to make it resemble a Tailor's Shop.
- If you don't have a toy sewing machine, make one with wooden blocks. Use three blocks—one long rectangle, one medium-size rectangle, and one square block. Stack them on top of each other, with the largest on the bottom, the smallest in the middle, and the medium-sized on the top. Cut out black knobs and dials and tape them on the machine. Use half a drinking straw for the needle.
- Show the children how to move material or clothes along the bottom block to "sew" them.

What to Do
* Tell the children that a tailor is someone who makes or fixes clothes. Talk about the tools tailors use, such as a sewing machine, a needle and thread, scissors, a measuring tape, an ironing board, and an iron.
* Set large dolls in the center and let children pretend to be tailors, making clothes for the dolls to wear.

Extension Idea
Let the children use plastic needles and yarn to sew designs on burlap squares.

Vocabulary
button
iron
ironing board
measuring tape
needle
sew
sewing machine
spool of thread
tailor
thread
zipper

Materials
buttons
burlap
dolls
iron
ironing board
large plastic needles
measuring tape
pieces of fabric
spools of thread
toy sewing machine
zippers

Click on the *Between the Lions* website!
pbskids.org/lions/gryphonhouse

Story: Joseph Had a Little Overcoat

PRETEND AND PLAY CENTER

Dress-Up Clothes

Skill Focus
Cooperation
Imaginative Play
Speaking and Communicating

Theme Connections
Celebrations
Clothing
Food

Vocabulary

china
elegant
fancy
jewelry
mirror

saucer
tea
tea party
teapot

Materials

dress-up clothes for boys and
    girls (hats, jewelry, scarves,
    and shoes)
Ella Sarah Gets Dressed by
    Margaret Chodos-Irvine or
    books that have pictures of
    children at a tea party or at
    another dress-up occasion
full-length mirror
hand-held mirror
plastic teacups and saucers
play food
tablecloth

What to Do

✳ Have a tea party! Explain that at a tea party, people dress in their nicest clothes, hats, and jewelry. Fancy foods are served, and guests may drink tea or juice from special dishes called china.

✳ Share books that have pictures of children at a tea party or at other dress-up occasion, such as *Ella Sarah Gets Dressed*.

✳ Show the children the illustration of the tea party on the last page of *Ella Sarah Gets Dressed*. Have the children use the materials to dress up and have a tea party. Talk with the children about the clothes they are wearing.

✳ Invite the children to engage in dramatic play: setting an elegant table for their tea party, dressing in their finest dress-up clothes, and joining their friends for some imaginary tea and snacks.

Extension Idea

Stand a full-length mirror in a corner. Let the children view themselves in the mirror. Show them how to use hand mirrors to see what they look like from the back.

Click on the *Between the Lions* website!
pbskids.org/lions/gryphonhouse
Video Clip: Blending Bowl: tea

Skill Focus
Creative Expression
Fine Motor Skills

Theme Connections
Clothing
Shapes

Spools

What to Do

* Fill the sand table with empty thread, yarn, and ribbon spools in a variety of sizes.
* Show the children how to roll the spools through the sand to make straight lines, curvy lines, zigzag lines, and wavy lines. Let the children make interesting designs and patterns by rolling the spools through the sand.
* Encourage the children to experiment with the spools in the sand. Can they make different kinds of lines? What can they build with the spools? Can the spools be used to sift the sand? Which spools sift sand the fastest? Why?
* Ask, *How can you use the end of the spool to make imprints in the sand? What shape is the imprint?*

Extension Idea

On another day, add some water to the sand to make it very damp. Let the children repeat the spool activities with wet sand.

Vocabulary

curvy	spool
imprint	straight
lines	wavy
sand	zigzag
sift	

Materials

empty thread, yarn, and ribbon
  spools
sand
sand table
water

Letter Molds ("Vv")

AGE 4+

Skill Focus
Fine Motor Skills

Letter Recognition

Theme Connections
The Alphabet

Clothing

Vocabulary

curvy	mold
first	sand
letter	straight
line	trace
lowercase	uppercase

Materials
index cards

plastic letter molds

sand

sand table

Preparation
• Write the uppercase and lowercase "Vv" on an index card to create a letter "Vv" card.

• Draw or cut out and paste a picture of a vest on an index card. Write the word *vest* below the picture to create a word card.

What to Do

✳ Select one letter of the alphabet. Focus on a letter that relates to a piece of clothing the children have learned about. In this case, the letter "Vv" is the example.

✳ Display the letter "Vv" card, and trace over the straight lines to show how the letters are formed.

✳ Encourage the children to write uppercase (big) "V" and lowercase (little) "v" in the sand.

✳ Then have the children press molds for the letters "V" and "v" into the sand to make raised letters. Have them trace the letters with their fingers.

✳ Say, *You made the letters "Vv"! It's the first letter in the word* vest. Have the children point out the "v" on the word card for *vest*.

✳ Ask the children if the uppercase "V" and the lowercase "v" are the same or different.

✳ Add new letter cards, word cards, pictures, and letter molds to the center. You might use:

| "Hh" *hat* | "Ss" *sock* | "Pp" *pants* |
| "Bb" *belt* | "Jj" *jacket* | "Mm" *mittens* |

Extension Idea
Repeat the activity, focusing on the last letter in the words *jacket, hat, belt,* and *vest*.

Skill Focus

Beginning Writing

Concepts of Print (Illustrations
    Carry Meaning)

Story Sequence

Theme Connections

All About Me

Clothing

Getting Dressed Book

AGE 3+

Preparation

• Make blank books by folding sheets of white paper in half. Each book will be four pages (one sheet of paper).

What to Do

⬚ Have the children pantomime getting dressed. Talk about the order of the steps as they act them out.

⬚ Let the children make books about getting dressed. Ask questions to help the children plan the story. *Who is getting dressed? What will that person put on first? Next? Last?*

⬚ Help the children write titles and their names on the cover of their books.

⬚ Tell them to draw and write their stories on the other pages. The children may wish to make wordless books. If they choose to write text, accept scribbles, letter-like symbols, letters, and attempts at words.

Extension Idea

Invite the children to share their books with the class. Point out the name of the author and illustrator on each book.

Vocabulary

author	last
book	next
cover	order
first	title
illustrator	

Materials

crayons

markers

paper

pencils

Click on the *Between the Lions* website!
pbskids.org/lions/gryphonhouse

Story: Ethan and the Snow

Skill Focus

Beginning Writing

Concepts of Print (Print Conveys Meaning, Spaces Between Words)

Creative Expression

Theme Connections

All About Me | Clothing

AGE 4+ T-Shirts

Vocabulary

characters	spaces
letters	T-shirt
message	writing
place	

Materials

construction paper

crayons

markers

pencils

scissors

T-shirts with a message

Preparation

• Cut T-shirt-shaped patterns from large sheets of construction paper.

• String a clothesline across the back of the Writing Center. Hang from the clothesline real T-shirts with writing and graphics on them.

What to Do

✳ Ask the children wearing T-shirts with writing or graphics on them to stand up. Read the words on the T-shirts together and talk about how the pictures go with the words. You might say, *Molly's T-shirt has a bunny on it. The words under the bunny say "Somebunny loves me!" The words tell me about the bunny.*

✳ Say, *Sometimes shirts tell about a special place you've visited or show a character or person that you like. Some shirts have colorful designs and words that make you happy.*

✳ Let each child draw pictures and write words to decorate a paper T-shirt. Some children may want to dictate and have you write their words. Talk about each letter as you write, and point out the spaces you leave between words.

✳ Hang the T-shirts on the clothesline.

Extension Idea

Invite each child to show and to read his or her T-shirt to the class.

CHAPTER 4

Colors

This topic allows the children to develop color recognition skills through hands-on activities, games, stories, and songs that encourage them to match, identify, and name colors. The children learn to mix primary colors to make a new color and write rhymes about the colors they see around them.

Rainbow Song
(Tune: "Twinkle, Twinkle, Little Star")

Red and orange,
Green and blue,
Lemon yellow, violet, too.
All the colors that we love
Paint a rainbow up above.

AGE 3+

ABC CENTER

A Rainbow of Letters

Skill Focus
Compare and Contrast
Letter Recognition
Vocabulary

Theme Connections
The Alphabet
Colors

Vocabulary

circle	match
colors	rainbow
curvy	slanted
letter	straight
line	trace

Materials

chart paper
crayons or markers
paint
paintbrushes
plastic letters

Preparation

- Draw a large rainbow onto chart paper. Color or paint each band with the appropriate color: red, orange, yellow, green, blue, violet. On each band, write the color word and the beginning letter:

green "Gg"	red "Rr"	yellow "Yy"
orange "Oo"	blue "Bb"	violet "Vv"

What to Do

✳ Sing the "Rainbow Song" to the tune of "Twinkle, Twinkle, Little Star." Have a volunteer point to the colors on the rainbow as the children sing the name of the color.

Rainbow Song
Red and orange,
Green and blue,
Lemon yellow, violet, too.
All the colors that we love
Paint a rainbow up above.

✳ Place the letters "Gg," "Rr," "Yy," "Oo," "Bb," and "Vv" onto a table. Have the children find the plastic letter that matches the first letter in the word *green*.

✳ Suggest that the children trace the plastic letter with their fingers as they say the name of the letter and describe how the letter looks. Ask, *Does it have straight lines, slanted lines, curvy lines, or circles?*

Click on the *Between the Lions* website!
pbskids.org/lions/gryphonhouse
Story: Spicy Hot Colors
Video Clip: Colorful Foods

Skill Focus

Letter Recognition

Vocabulary

Theme Connections

The Alphabet

Colors

Letter Search ("Rr," "Yy," "Bb")

AGE 3+

Preparation

- Prepare three pieces of poster paper. Write either "Rr," "Yy," or "Bb," at the top. Write the letter "Rr" with a red marker, "Yy" with yellow marker, and "Bb" with blue.

What to Do

- ✳ Show the children three pieces of paper, each with a letter heading—"Rr," "Yy," or "Bb."
- ✳ Have the children search through flyers, magazines, and newspapers to find and then cut out the letters "Rr," "Yy," and "Bb" and objects that are red, yellow, or blue.
- ✳ Help them paste the letters onto the appropriate poster. Look at and talk about the completed posters together.

Extension Idea

Use the same approach for other letters of the alphabet that are the beginning letters of color words, including "Gg," "Oo," and "Pp." Tell the children that the color *green* begins with the letter "g," *orange* begin with "o," and *purple* begins with "p."

Vocabulary

big	lowercase
colors	search
find	small
letter	uppercase

Materials

advertisement flyers,
   magazines, and newspapers

glue sticks

magazines

newspapers

scissors

three pieces of poster paper

Click on the *Between the Lions* website!
pbskids.org/lions/gryphonhouse

Poem: Yellow

Games: ABCD Watermelon
      Sky Riding

ART CENTER
Color Collage

AGE 3+

Skill Focus
Color Recognition
Creative Expression
Vocabulary

Theme Connections
Colors
Shapes

Vocabulary

blue	red
circle	square
collage	triangle
color words	yellow

Materials

art scraps (crepe paper,
    pictures, ribbon, yarn)
construction paper
crayons
glitter
glue
markers
small red objects (for example:
    buttons, beads, milk caps)

Preparation
• Cut circles, squares, triangles, hearts, and stars from red construction paper.

What to Do

❋ Explain that a collage is a piece of art made by gluing different objects and shapes onto a piece of paper.

❋ Have the children make collages by selecting only red objects and shapes, arranging them onto a piece of construction paper, and then gluing the objects and shapes into place.

❋ The children can fill in the open spaces on the paper by drawing with red crayons or markers. Older children may want to draw squiggly lines with a glue stick and sprinkle red glitter over them.

❋ When the children have completed the collages, ask them to name the different shapes and objects. Help them write their names on the collages—with a red marker of course!

Extension Ideas

❋ In the days that follow, have the children make collages, each featuring a different color.

❋ Post the collages on a bulletin board, or frame them with colored construction paper and make an art exhibit for the school, public library, or another public place.

Click on the *Between the Lions* website!
pbskids.org/lions/gryphonhouse

Stories: Spicy Hot Colors
POP POP POP POP POP

Skill Focus

Color Recognition

Creative Expression

Theme Connections

Colors

Shapes

Sponge Painting

AGE
3+

Preparation

- Cut sponges into different shapes and sizes. Wet them and squeeze out the excess water.
- Place a small amount of paint into each section of the egg carton.

What to Do

✴ Have the children choose among the sponge shapes. They may want to clip clothespins to the sponges to use as handles.

✴ Have the children dip the sponges into the paint and dab them onto paper as many times as they wish.

✴ Encourage them to continue, using sponges of different shapes and sizes.

Extension Idea

Ask the children to name the different colors in their sponge paintings. Help the children write their names on their paintings.

Vocabulary

black	purple
blue	red
brown	sponge
circle	square
green	triangle
orange	yellow

Materials

clothespins

foam egg cartons

paint

paper

scissors

smocks

sponges

Click on the Between the Lions website!

pbskids.org/lions/gryphonhouse

Story: Elephants Can Paint Too!

Video Clip: Colorful Foods

ART CENTER

Marble Painting

Skill Focus

Beginning Writing (Names)
Color Recognition
Creative Expression

Theme Connections

Colors
Creativity

Vocabulary

color words   painting
lid   roll
marble   tilt

Materials

cups or other small containers
marbles
paint
paper
shallow box or box lid (about
    the size of the paper)
spoons

Preparation

- Fill three cups with different paint colors. Put a marble and a spoon into each cup.
- Line the bottom of a box lid with white paper.

What to Do

❋ Have the children choose a color to start the marble painting. Show them how to use the spoon to scoop the marble out of the paint cup. Place the marble onto the paper inside the box lid.

❋ Have the children tilt the box into different directions so the marble rolls around, making lines of paint across the paper.

❋ When the children finish with a marble, encourage them to gently drop it back into the matching paint cup and then choose a different marble and color to use.

Note: Remind the children to keep marbles out of their mouths.

Extension Idea

Ask the children to name the different colors in their marble paintings. Help them write their names onto their creations.

Click on the *Between the Lions* website!
pbskids.org/lions/gryphonhouse
Story: Elephants Can Paint Too!

Skill Focus

Environmental Print

Hand-Eye Coordination

Imaginative Play

Vocabulary

Theme Connections

Colors

Communities | Transportation

Road Signs

AGE 4+

Preparation

- Use colored poster board and markers to make road signs that have distinct and meaningful shapes and colors: red stop sign, yellow yield sign, green campground area sign, yellow railroad crossing sign, red do-not-enter sign, and a red, yellow, and green traffic light.

What to Do

- ⊞ Show the children the poster board signs. Have the children describe the shape and color of each sign. Explain that the signs also have letters and words that tell drivers what to do. Discuss what each sign means. Then post the signs in the Block Center.
- ⊞ Have the children build roads using building blocks. Invite them to create road signs to place along the roads.
- ⊞ The children can draw the road signs on index cards. Help them cut out the signs and tape them to wooden craft sticks.
- ⊞ Fill bottle caps with clay. Press the craft sticks into the clay to make bases for the signs.
- ⊞ Let the children place the signs and move toy vehicles along the roadways.

Extension Idea

Visit the Block Center and observe the children as they build and play. Talk about the colors and shapes of the different signs and what they mean.

Vocabulary

bus	shapes
car	square
circle	train
colors	triangle
green	truck
red	yellow
road signs	

Materials

bottle caps

building blocks

index cards

markers

modeling clay

poster board

tape

toy vehicles

wooden craft sticks

AGE 3+

Book-Browsing for Colors

Skill Focus
Book Care and Handling
Choosing Books
Concepts of Print

Theme Connections
All About Me
Colors

Vocabulary

author	label
characters	pictures
colors	read
cover	return
illustration	title

Materials

fiction and nonfiction books about colors (See pages 219–220 for suggestions.)

markers

paper

scissors

tape or glue

Preparation

- Set up browsing boxes with a variety of books about colors. Include both fiction and nonfiction titles.
- Create a written label for each book-browsing box.
- Cut out a large colored rectangle that relates to each book-browsing topic, and put this next to the written label, so the children know the kind of books that are in each box.
- For this theme, you might have book-browsing boxes for red, yellow, blue, green, brown, orange, and one for multiple colors.

What to Do

✳ Explain to the children that the labels on the book-browsing boxes will help them select the kind of book they want to read and will also help them put the book away.

✳ Ask, *If you want to read about how an artist mixes colors, which box would you look in?* (The box decorated with all of the colors.) *When you have finished the book* Brown Bear, Brown Bear, *where will you put it?* (In the box with a brown label.)

✳ Encourage the children to select books that interest them and to look at the words and illustrations on their own or with a friend.

✳ Model looking at a book cover to predict what the book will be about and then turning the pages to "read" it.

Click on the *Between the Lions* website!
pbskids.org/lions/gryphonhouse

Stories: Spicy Hot Colors
Yesterday I Had the Blues
Song: Got a Good Reason to Read

Skill Focus

Book Appreciation

Choosing Books

Comprehension (Characters, Predicting)

Theme Connections

All About Me

Colors | Families

Color Books

AGE
3+

Preparation

• Fill the Library Center with fiction books about colors. Include books with repeated and predictable text.

What to Do

❋ Read aloud a book with predictable text, such as *The Little Red Hen* or *Who Said Red?*

❋ After the pattern of the story has been established, invite the children to chime in on the repeated phrases or to complete predictable patterns. You might read, *Who will help me grind the wheat?* Pause to let the children look at the illustrations and complete the sentences: "_____," *said the Cat.* "_____," *said the Dog.* "_____," *said the Duck.*

❋ Point to the illustrations in the book to help clarify which character is speaking and to give clues to the meaning of unfamiliar words, such as *seeds, wheat, grind, flour, mill,* and *wheelbarrow.*

❋ Say, *I wonder what will happen next?* Encourage the children to "read" the book to find out.

❋ Invite the children to select other books that interest them and to look at the words and the pictures on their own or with another child.

Extension Idea

On another day, invite the children to use their favorite colors to draw pictures of one of the characters in the books.

Vocabulary

cover	predict
flour	seeds
grind	title
illustration	wheat
mill	wheelbarrow
pattern	words

Materials

crayons

drawing paper

The Little Red Hen by Paul Galdone, Jerry Pinkney, and others, *Who Said Red?* by Mary Serfozo, or other fiction books related to colors (See pages 219–220 for suggestions.)

Click on the *Between the Lions* website!

pbskids.org/lions/gryphonhouse

Story: The Little Red Hen

AGE **3+**

Color Sorting

Skill Focus

Compare and Contrast

Sorting

Theme Connections

Colors

Opposites (Same and Different)

Vocabulary

alike	graph
color	same
color words	sort
different	

Materials

red, blue, and green objects
(small blocks, large buttons,
milk caps, toys)

red, blue, and green trays or
boxes

Preparation

• Place red, blue, and green objects on a table. Set out sorting trays or boxes of matching colors.

What to Do

❋ Provide time for free play and exploration, letting the children observe and discuss the objects in their own way.

❋ Invite the children to sort the objects. Think aloud as you demonstrate how to sort. Say, *I am going to sort these objects by their color. What color is this block? It's red. I am going to take this red block and put it on the red tray. Who can find another object that is red? Where does it go? Yes, it belongs on the red tray with the red block.*

❋ Let the children sort the blue and green objects on their own.

❋ Suggest that after the children finish sorting the objects, they mix up the objects so this activity is ready for the next child or group of children.

Extension Idea

Help the children make a pictograph showing the numbers of red, blue, and green objects.

Click on the *Between the Lions* website!
pbskids.org/lions/gryphonhouse

Story: POP POP POP POP POP

Game: The Messy Attic

Skill Focus
Cause and Effect
Mix Colors
Observe Changes

Theme Connections
Colors
Creativity

Color Mixing

AGE 4+

Preparation
- Set out jars of red, yellow, and blue fingerpaint. Put a spoon into each jar.

What to Do
- ✳ Discuss that when two colors are mixed together, a new color is created.
- ✳ Scoop a spoonful of yellow fingerpaint and put it onto your paper. Beside it, put a spoonful of blue paint. Have the children identify the two colors.
- ✳ Put one hand into each paint color, and begin to make circles across the paper. Ask, *What do you think will happen if I mix the yellow and blue paint?* Overlap the circles to mix the paint. Explain that when yellow and blue are mixed they make green.
- ✳ Let the children experiment with different color combinations as they fingerpaint. Invite them to share their discoveries with others.

Extension Idea
Color mixing can be done in many different ways. The children can mix paint in cups, on paper, or in zip-top bags. They can also mix different colors of modeling clay or shaving cream that you have colored with food coloring. Try some experiments.

Vocabulary
blue	orange
fingerpaint	purple
green	red
mix	yellow

Materials
fingerpaint
fingerpaint paper
plastic spoons

Click on the *Between the Lions* website!
pbskids.org/lions/gryphonhouse

Story: Elephants Can Paint Too!
Poem: Fingerpaints

PRETEND AND PLAY CENTER

Traffic Light

Skill Focus
Cooperation
Identifying Colors
Imaginative Play

Theme Connections
Colors
My Community

Vocabulary
go
green
red
slow

stop
traffic light
vehicle
yellow

Materials
markers
masking tape
poster board

Preparation
- Make three large traffic lights. Draw and cut out a traffic light from poster board. Color in a different circle on each traffic light so that one has the red light, one has the yellow light, and one has the green light.
- Use masking tape to make a road that winds around the learning center.

What to Do
❋ Sing "Traffic Light" with the children to the tune of "The Wheels on the Bus."

Traffic Light
The colors on the light turn
Green, yellow, red,
Green, yellow, red,
Green, yellow, red.
The colors on the light turn
Green, yellow, red,
All around the town.

❋ Hold up the traffic lights and explain what each color tells the driver to do (go, slow down, stop).
❋ Have the children pretend to drive cars, trucks, or buses on the busy streets in the learning center. One child can hold up one traffic light at a time, a signal to the drivers to go, slow down, or stop their vehicles.

Extension Idea
Take photos of the children in the learning center. Post the photos and have the children dictate captions.

Skill Focus
Creative Expression
Retelling a Story

Theme Connections
Colors
Creativity

Act Out Colors

AGE 4+

What to Do

⚹ Read a book about colors, such as *Red Sings from Treetops: A Year in Colors* by Joyce Sidman or *Spicy Hot Colors: Colores Picantes* by Sherry Shanahan, to the children.

⚹ Ask questions such as these to help the children recall the events in the story: *What happens first? What happens next?*

⚹ Have the children act out the story, and then encourage them to act out how one of colors makes them feel. The children can put on costumes and use props from the prop box.

Extension Idea

The children can sing the "Rainbow Song" to the tune of "Twinkle, Twinkle, Little Star" as they act out how colors make them feel.

Rainbow Song
Red and orange,
Green and blue,
Lemon yellow, violet too.
All the colors that we love
Paint a rainbow up above.
Red and orange,
Green and blue,
Lemon yellow, violet too.

Vocabulary
act out   feelings
color words

Materials
fiction and nonfiction books about colors, such as *Red Sings from Treetops: A Year in Colors* by Joyce Sidman or *Spicy Hot Colors: Colores Picantes* by Sherry Shanahan
props (costumes, hats, scarves, boots in different colors)

Click on the *Between the Lions* website!
pbskids.org/lions/gryphonhouse

Stories: Spicy Hot Colors
        Yesterday I Had the Blues
Poem: Yellow

Skill Focus

Fine Motor Skills

Letter Recognition

Letter Molds "Rr"

Theme Connections

The Alphabet

Colors

Vocabulary

curvy	name
first	sand
letter	straight
line	trace
lowercase	uppercase
mold	

Materials

index cards

plastic letter molds

sand

sand table

Preparation

- Write the uppercase and lowercase "Rr" onto an index card to create a letter "Rr" card.
- Draw or cut out and paste a picture of a red crayon onto an index card. Write the word *red* below the picture to create a word card for red.

What to Do

* Select one letter of the alphabet. Focus on a letter that relates to a color the children are reading stories about. In this case, the letter "Rr" is the example.

* Display the letter "Rr" card, and trace over the straight lines and the curvy lines to show how the letters are formed.

* Encourage the children to write an uppercase (big) "R" and lowercase (little) "r" in the sand. Then, have the children press molds for the letters "R" and "r" into the sand to make raised letters. Have them trace the letters with their fingers.

* Ask the children if the uppercase and lowercase letters are the same or different.

* Say, *You made the letter "Rr"! It's the first letter in the color word* red. Have the children point out the "r" on the word card for *red*.

* Add new letter cards, word cards, and pictures to the center.

Click on the *Between the Lions* website!

pbskids.org/lions/gryphonhouse

Story: The Little Red Hen

Song: Upper and Lowercase

Games: Theo's Puzzles (r)

Skill Focus

Beginning Writing

Concepts of Print

Rhyming

Theme Connections

Colors

Sounds

Color Rhymes

AGE
4+

What to Do

✻ Sing "Oh, Do You Know Two Rhyming Words?" to the tune of "Do You Know the Muffin Man?"

Oh, Do You Know Two Rhyming Words?

Oh, do you know two rhyming words,

Two rhyming words,

Two rhyming words?

Oh, do you know two rhyming words?

They sound a lot alike.

Red and *bed* are rhyming words,

Two rhyming words,

Two rhyming words.

Red and *bed* are rhyming words.

They sound a lot alike.

✻ Use white chalk to write this pattern onto a piece of red paper: red and _____

✻ Have the children think of other words that rhyme with *red*, such as *head*. Model how to write the word *head* on the line and have a volunteer draw a picture to go with it.

✻ Use white chalk to write this pattern onto a piece of black paper: black and _____

✻ Have the children copy the pattern and then write a word or draw a picture of something that rhymes with the word *black*. Accept scribbles, symbols, letters, or complete words.

Vocabulary

alike   rhyme

pairs   tune

pattern

Materials

black and red papers

chalk

marker

Click on the *Between the Lions* website!
pbskids.org/lions/gryphonhouse

Story: Spicy Hot Colors

Game: Dub Cubs

WRITING CENTER

Our Favorite Colors

Skill Focus
Beginning Writing
Concepts of Print

Theme Connections
All About Me
Colors

Vocabulary

blue   purple
favorite   red
green   yellow
orange

Material

colored paper
crayons
drawing paper
glue stick
hole punch
markers
yarn

Preparation

• Cut 2″ x 6″ strips of colored paper, enough for each child to have one of each color. On each strip, write the word that names that color.

What to Do

✶ Ask the children, *What is your favorite color—the color you like best of all?* As the children name colors, have each of them choose a strip of paper in that color. Tell them that the word for that color is written on the strip. Look at the letters in the words and then read them together.

✶ The children should glue the color strips on the top of their drawing papers.

✶ Ask the children to draw pictures of objects in their favorite colors.

✶ Help the children write their names at the bottom of their papers. Remind them to leave a space between each letter and to begin the name with an uppercase letter.

✶ Combine the pages to make a class book. Write the title "Our Favorite Colors" on the cover.

Extension Idea

Challenge the children to trace over the letters in the color word and then write them on the page.

Click on the Between the Lions website!
pbskids.org/lions/gryphonhouse
Stories: POP POP POP POP POP
Yesterday I Had the Blues
Video Clip: Colorful Foods

88 **WILD ABOUT** LEARNING CENTERS

Families

Talking with the children in your classroom about their families is a wonderful way to learn about the children and for them to learn about one another. As the children pretend to sort and wash clothes, rock babies, and draw pictures of their families, they learn new words and concepts and discover similarities and differences between themselves and others.

Going Shopping

Come go to the store with me,
It's just down the street.
We don't need a car,
We can go on our feet.
Daddy wants apples
And onions and steak,
Mother wants bread
And strawberry cake.
Brother wants chicken
And fish and potatoes,
I want cereal
And lettuce and tomatoes.

Come go to the store with me,
It's just down the street.
We don't need a car,
We can go on our feet.

ABC CENTER

AGE 3+

Letter Match

Skill Focus
Letter Recognition

Theme Connections
All About Me

The Alphabet

Families

Vocabulary

circle	match
curvy	slanted
first name	straight
letter	trace
lowercase	uppercase

Materials

blank index cards

markers

plastic uppercase letters

Preparation

- Make a name card for each child by writing their names on index cards, using uppercase letters for the initial letters and lowercase letters for the remaining letters.

What to Do

✳ On a table, arrange the name cards and plastic uppercase letters that correspond to the first letters in the children's first names.

✳ The children hunt for the plastic letter that matches the first letter on their name card.

✳ Suggest that the children trace the plastic letters with their fingers as they say the name of the letter and describe how the letter looks. Ask, *Does it have straight lines, slanted lines, curvy lines, or circles?*

Extension Idea

Have each child say aloud the first letter in her name. Tell the children the sound that the letter makes. Say, *Betsy, your name begins with the letter "B." The letter "B" makes the /b/ sound. Let's say it together—/b/. Byron and Bella also have names that begin with the /b/ sound!*

Click on the *Between the Lions* website!
pbskids.org/lions/gryphonhouse

Song: Upper and Lowercase
Game: Theo's Puzzles

Skill Focus
Letter Recognition

Theme Connections
The Alphabet
Families

Alphabet Sponges "Kk," "Ll," "Nn," "Oo"

AGE 3+

Preparation
- Write the uppercase and lowercase letters "Kk," "Ll," "Nn," and "Qq" on a chart. Post the chart in the ABC Center.
- If you do not have letter sponges, cut sponges to make the letters "Kk," "Ll," "Nn," and "Oo." Wet the letters and squeeze out the excess water.
- Place a small amount of poster paint into shallow foam trays.

What to Do
※ Read books about alphabet letters, such as *The Letters Are Lost!* Look for the letters "Kk," "Ll," "Nn," and "Oo" in the book. Name the letters and describe how each is formed.
※ Have each child choose a sponge letter. Show them how to press the sponge letter into the paint and then onto the paper to make a print.
※ Invite the children to match their stamped letters to the letters on the alphabet chart or to the corresponding letter page in one of the alphabet books.
※ Encourage them to continue using sponges with different uppercase and lowercase letters.

Vocabulary
alphabet	match
corresponding	shapes
letters	sponge
lowercase	uppercase

Materials
alphabet sponges
drawing paper
foam trays
The Letters Are Lost! by Lisa Campbell Ernst or another alphabet book (See page 217 for suggestions.)
poster paint
poster board

Click on the *Between the Lions* website!
pbskids.org/lions/gryphonhouse

Song: Library A to Z
Games: ABCD Watermelon
　　　　 Sky Riding

ART CENTER

Stuffed Animals

AGE 3+

Skill Focus
Creative Expression
Fine Motor Skills
Sharing Ideas and Feelings

Theme Connections
All About Me
Families
Feelings

Vocabulary

color
cuddly
describe
draw
eyes

favorite
legs
shape
stuffed animal
tail

Materials

art scraps (bows, buttons,
    ribbon, yarn)
crayons
drawing paper
glue
Knuffle Bunny by Mo Willems
markers

What to Do

* Talk about books you've read in which one of the family members has a stuffed animal. For example, say, *Remember Trixie in the book* Knuffle Bunny? *What is Trixie's favorite stuffed animal?* (Knuffle Bunny!)
* Connect the book to the children by asking, *Do you have a favorite stuffed animal? Think about what it looks like. What color is it? What shape is it? Does it have eyes? Legs? A tail?*
* Have the children draw a picture of their favorite stuffed animal. Let them glue ribbons, bows, buttons, and other art scraps onto the picture to add details.
* Ask the children to talk to you about their drawings. *Your stuffed animal looks so cuddly. What's its name?*

Extension Idea

Help children write their names on their drawings. Offer to write the name of the stuffed animal on the picture, too.

Click on the *Between the Lions* website!
pbskids.org/lions/gryphonhouse
Song: Grubby Pup

Skill Focus

Creative Expression

Fine Motor Skills

Hand-Eye Coordination

Theme Connections

All About Me

Families

ART CENTER

Family Pictures

AGE 3+

Preparation

- Purchase paints in a variety of skin tones or mix your own paints. Add these colors to the Art Center.

What to Do

* Have the children paint pictures of their families. Some of the children may want to paint two separate pictures if their parents live in different locations.

* Encourage the children to talk about the people (and pets) in their picture. Say, *I like your painting. Where are you in the picture? Who is that next to you? Is this kitten part of your family? What is its name?*

* Help the children write or paint their first name and their family (last) name on their pictures.

Extension Idea

Make a mural in the room by connecting all of the individual family paintings. Use the mural to discuss families and how each is unique.

Vocabulary

brother   grandpa

family   mother

father   sister

grandma

Materials

easel

large paper

markers

paint

paintbrushes

smocks

Click on the Between the Lions website!

pbskids.org/lions/gryphonhouse

Story: My Dog Is as Smelly as Dirty Socks

Video Clips: Family Portrait

I Love My Family

AGE 3+

My Home

Skill Focus
Hand-Eye Coordination
Maintaining Concentration
Vocabulary

Theme Connections
All About Me
Families
Homes and Houses

Vocabulary
bathe	house
bedroom	people
build	structure
family	upstairs
home	

Materials
building blocks
camera (optional)
nonfiction books about houses
   (See page 223 for
   suggestions.)
   and families (See page 220
   for suggestions.)
plastic family figures

What to Do
✳ Challenge the children to use the blocks to build a home for their family. Suggest that they think about how many bedrooms they will need, where the family will eat and bathe, and if they want a one-story home or a home with an upstairs.

✳ Observe the children as they play with blocks and family figures. Ask them to describe the structures they are building, who the family figures are, and what they are doing. Ask question such as, *What are you building? Tell me about the home. Who lives there? What is the family doing?*

Extension Idea
Take photographs of the children with their structures. Post the photographs on the wall in the Block Center.

Click on the *Between the Lions* website!
pbskids.org/lions/gryphonhouse
Story: Castles, Caves, and Honeycombs
Song: My House
Video Clip: Cliff Hanger Sells His House

Skill Focus

Hand-Eye Coordination

Vocabulary

Theme Connections

Families

Neighborhoods

Our Neighborhood

AGE 4+

Preparation

- Place masking tape on the floor in the shape of a "t" to create the streets in the make-believe neighborhood. Place lines on the outside of the "t" to create sidewalks.

What to Do

- ✳ Explain that a neighborhood is the place where people live and work. Look at pictures of neighborhoods in familiar books such as *Knuffle Bunny* and *Jonathan and His Mommy*. Point out streets, sidewalks, houses, buildings, and parks in the pictures. Talk about the buildings and what they're used for (laundromat, library, post office, and so on).
- ✳ Invite the children to work together to build a block neighborhood.
- ✳ The children may add small plastic figures of people and toy vehicles to help the neighborhood come alive with activity.
- ✳ Ask, *Where are the girl and her father going? What are they going to do there? What will they pass on their way to the library? to the laundromat?*

Extension Idea

Help the children make labels for the buildings and places in the neighborhood.

Vocabulary

block	post office
laundromat	sidewalk
library	store
neighborhood	street
park	

Materials

building blocks

Jonathan and His Mommy by Irene Smalls, *Knuffle Bunny* by Mo Willems, or other books about neighborhoods (See page 220 for suggestions.)

labels

pencils

toy people

toy vehicles

Family Books

AGE 3+

Skill Focus
Book Care and Handling
Choosing Books
Concepts of Print

Theme Connections
All About Me
Families
Neighborhoods

Vocabulary

author   illustration
cover   predict
care for   title
handle

Materials

fiction and nonfiction books about families (See page 220 for suggestions.)

Preparation

• Fill the Library Center with nonfiction books about different kinds of families. Include books about the people who make up a family, where people live, and what they do together.

What to Do

✳ Encourage the children to select books that interest them and to look at the words and the pictures on their own or with another child.

✳ Model how to look at the illustrations on a book cover, predict what the book will be about, and decide whether you want to read it. Say, *This book has a picture of a girl holding a baby on the cover. I think it's her baby sister. Don't you have a baby sister, Lea? You might like to read this book.*

✳ Demonstrate how to hold, handle, and care for a book.

✳ Show the children where to begin reading and how to turn the pages. Read parts of the book aloud. Pause to discuss the factual information in the book.

✳ Help the children make connections to new books. You might say, *You've picked another book by Irene Smalls. This one is called* Kevin and His Dad. *Look at the pictures and see what Kevin and his Dad do together.*

Click on the *Between the Lions* website!
pbskids.org/lions/gryphonhouse
Story: My Dog Is as Smelly as Dirty Socks
Song: Read a Book Today!

Skill Focus

Book Appreciation

Choosing Books

Concepts of Print

Theme Connections

All About Me

Families

Family Favorites

AGE 3+

Preparation

- Fill the Library Center with fiction books about families. Include books with repeated and predictable text.

What to Do

⊠ Read aloud a book with predictable text, such as *Waddle, Waddle, Quack, Quack, Quack*. Invite the children to participate in the reading by making the sounds of the animals in this duck family.

⊠ After the pattern of the story has been established, pause to let the children "read" the sound words or to complete predictable patterns. Pause at the appropriate places to let the children look at the illustrations and complete the sentence: *Waddle, waddle, quack, quack, quack.*

⊠ Say, *I wonder what will happen next?* Encourage the children to "read" the book to find out.

⊠ Invite the children to select other books that interest them and to look at the words and the pictures on their own or with another child.

Vocabulary

cover	quack
crack	tap
illustration	title
pattern	waddle
predict	words

Materials

Waddle, Waddle, Quack, Quack, Quack by Barbara Anne Skalak or other fiction books about families (See page 220 for suggestions.)

Extension Idea

Invite the children to add motions, gestures, and sound effects that mirror those in the books such as tapping, cracking, waddling, and booming.

Click on the *Between the Lions* website!

pbskids.org/lions/gryphonhouse

Story: Just What Mama Needs

Video Clip: I Love My Family

MATH AND SCIENCE CENTER

Sorting Socks

AGE 3+

Skill Focus
Compare and Contrast
Observe and Describe
Sorting

Theme Connections
All About Me
Families
Opposites (Same and Different)

Vocabulary

alike	partner
color	same
color words	size
match	socks
mate	sort
pair	stripes

Materials
laundry basket
pairs of socks of different colors,
    sizes, and designs

What to Do

✳ Set out four pairs of socks, two adult-sized (one blue pair and one white pair) and two child-sized (one blue pair and one white pair). Have the children sort the socks by size, putting all the big socks side by side and all the little socks side by side. Then have them find the matching socks and put the partner on top of its mate.

✳ Now suggest that the children sort and match the same socks by color.

✳ Set out a laundry basket filled with socks and let the children sort and match the socks in different ways.

Extension Idea

Encourage the use of descriptive language by asking the children why the two socks match. Ask, *In what way are these two socks alike? Are they the same color? Are they the same size? Do they have the same stripes?*

Click on the *Between the Lions* website!
pbskids.org/lions/gryphonhouse

Games: The Messy Attic
Monkey Match

Skill Focus

Compare and Contrast

Observe and Describe

Share Ideas

Theme Connections

Animals

Families

MATH AND SCIENCE CENTER

Moms and Babies

AGE 3+

Preparation

- Gather pictures of baby animals (calf, kitten, puppy, chick, piglet, and others) and the corresponding mother animals (cow, cat, dog, hen, pig, and others). Glue each picture on a blank index card.

Vocabulary

baby	hen
calf	kitten
cat	mother
chick	pig
cow	piglet
dog	puppy

Materials

glue

index cards

pictures of baby animals

pictures of mother animals

scissors

What to Do

✳ Have partners play a game to match baby animals with their mothers.

✳ Have the children turn the picture cards face down on a table. One child turns over two cards and names the animals. If the animals are a match (the mother and baby from the same family), the child keeps the matching cards and turns over two new ones. Talk with the children about the match. Say, *Yes, that's the baby cat's mother. Do you know what a baby cat is called? It is called a kitten. Do you have a cat or a kitten at home?*

✳ If the cards do not match, the child turns them face down again and the partner takes a turn.

✳ Play continues until all of the cards have been matched.

Extension Idea

Begin with only three pairs of matching animals. Make the game more challenging by adding additional pairs of animal cards. With each set of new cards, introduce the animals and the correct name for the baby and the mother.

Click on the Between the Lions website!
pbskids.org/lions/gryphonhouse

Story: An Egg Is Quiet
Poem: Baby Chick

PRETEND AND PLAY CENTER

House Play

Skill Focus

Express Empathy and Caring

Imaginative Play

Listening and Speaking

Theme Connections

Families

Homes and Houses

Vocabulary

baby	hungry
chores	sleeping
cleaning	tired
clothes	warm
cooking	

Materials

house play materials (boy and girl baby dolls, plastic bottles, toy cribs, blankets, dishes, plastic food, pots, pans, baby food jars, and so on)

writing and drawing materials

Preparation

• Create a house play area. Add props and materials to the Pretend and Play Center so that it resembles a real home. The house play area is a great way to teach the children how to work together and help out with family chores.

What to Do

✳ Let the children explore the house play area. Invite them to use the props and materials in the center as they act out roles of different family members, dressing up, or performing family chores such as cooking, cleaning, and shopping.

✳ When you visit the center, talk with the children about what they are doing. Say, *I like the way you are holding the baby. Do you think the baby is cold? How can we keep him warm? You are taking such good care of the baby!*

Extension Idea

Promote math skills by encouraging the children to count and measure food as they prepare it for their family. Focus on early writing skills by suggesting that the children take notes, write phone numbers, or make shopping lists.

Click on the *Between the Lions* website!

pbskids.org/lions/gryphonhouse

Stories: Bee-bim Bop!

Just What Mama Needs

Skill Focus

Cooperation

Imaginative Play

Sequencing

Theme Connections

Clothing

Families

Washing Machine

AGE 3+

Preparation

- Cut an opening in the cardboard box to make a washing machine door that can open and close.
- Draw a big circle in the door for the "window."

What to Do

✳ Help the children make a pretend washing machine from a large cardboard box. Have them cut and paste pictures of clothes in the "window."

✳ The children can draw knobs and dials on the top of the machine. Write the word *Start* on one knob. Ask the children to listen to the beginning (and ending) sound in the word and tell you the letter that stands for that sound.

✳ Place the washing machine in the Pretend and Play Center. Talk with the children about who does the laundry at their houses. Ask, *Does that person use a washing machine? Wash the clothes in the sink? Go to a laundromat?*

✳ Encourage creative thinking and working together as the children play with the washing machine. Ask questions that focus on sequence, such as, *I see that you are filling the washing machine with clothes. How much detergent will you put in? How will you start the machine? What will you do with the clean clothes?*

Vocabulary

clean	laundromat
clothes	off
clothesline	on
clothing	start
detergent	washing
dirty	machine
dry	wet
laundry	

Materials

doll clothes

dolls

clothesline

clothespins

empty detergent box

large cardboard box

laundry basket

markers

plastic measuring cup

scissors

Click on the *Between the Lions* website!

pbskids.org/lions/gryphonhouse

Poem: Ode to the Washing Machine

Popcorn Popper

AGE 3+

Skill Focus
Communicating Ideas and Feelings
Gross Motor Skills
Imaginative Play

Theme Connections
Families
Food

Vocabulary
attach
instructions
knob
machine
outing
pop
popcorn
popcorn popper
start
stop

Materials
buttons
cardboard boxes and tubes
glue
packing peanuts or cotton balls
paint

Preparation
• Help the children make a popcorn popper by attaching cardboard boxes and tubes together. Decorate the popcorn popper and add knobs, on/off buttons, and a label that says "Popcorn 50¢."

What to Do

✳ Talk with the children about their favorite family outings. Ask if any of them like to go to the movies and get popcorn.

✳ Place the popcorn popper in the Pretend and Play Center. Have the children fill the machine with "popcorn" (packing peanuts, cotton balls, or scrunched up paper).

✳ Ask the children to explain how to use the machine. Write down their instructions, and attach them to the popcorn popper.

✳ As the children engage in dramatic play, encourage them to say the "Popcorn Chant" to start and stop the popcorn popper.

Popcorn Chant
Popcorn popper,
Pop, pop, pop!
Popcorn popper,
Do not stop!

Poppity, bobbity, pop, pop, pop,
Hoppity, poppity, hop, hop, hop.
Dop and a hoppity,
Lop and a doppity.
Pop and a hoppity.
Stop, pop, stop.

Skill Focus
Fine Motor Skills

Letter Recognition

Theme Connections
The Alphabet

Families

Letter Molds ("Dd")

AGE 4+

Preparation
- Write the uppercase and lowercase "Dd" on an index card to create a letter "Dd" card.
- Draw or cut out and paste a picture of a man on an index card. Write the word *Dad* below the picture to create a word card for Dad.

What to Do

❊ Select one letter of the alphabet. Focus on a letter that relates to families or names for people in a family. In this case, the letter "Dd" is the example.

❊ Display the letter "Dd" card and trace over the straight line and the curvy line to show how each letter is formed.

❊ Encourage the children to write uppercase "D" and lowercase "d" in the sand.

❊ Then have the children press molds for the letters "D" and "d" into the sand to make raised letters. Have them trace the letters with their fingers.

❊ Say, *You made the letter "D"! It's the first letter and the last letter in the word* Dad. Have the children point out the "d" on the word card for *Dad.*

❊ Add new letter cards, word cards, pictures, and letter molds to the center. You might use:

| "Mm" *Mom* | "Ff" *family* | "Gg" *Grandpa* |
| "Bb" *baby* | "Ss" *sister* | "Cc" *cat* |

Vocabulary
curvy	mold
first	sand
letter	straight
line	trace
lowercase	uppercase

Materials
index cards

plastic letter molds

sand

sand table

Click on the Between the Lions website!

pbskids.org/lions/gryphonhouse

Song: Upper and Lowercase

Video Clip: Blending Bowl: dine

Games: Monkey Match

WRITING CENTER

AGE **3+**

Stories That Bind

Concepts of Print

Creative Expressions

Early Writing

Theme Connections

All About Me

Families

Vocabulary

accordion	sister
brother	title
family	words
father	write
mother	

Materials

construction paper 12" x 18"

crayons

Knuffle Bunny by Mo Willems

pencils

scissors

Preparation

- Make an accordion book for each child. Fold a piece of 12" x 18" construction paper in half lengthwise and cut it along the fold into two long pieces, each 6"x18". Then fold the long strip, accordion-style, to make a three-section book.

What to Do

✳ Talk about the framed photos of Trixie's family on the title page of *Knuffle Bunny*. You might say, *Yes, this is a picture of Trixie's mom and dad taking a walk with her when she was a baby. Where do you think they are going?*

✳ Invite the children to tell you stories about something fun they did with their families.

✳ Have them draw pictures in their accordion books to show what happened first, next, and last.

✳ As the children share their stories, record the words they use on the corresponding pages of their books.

✳ Fold the books accordion-style and turn them over to show the blank covers. Write the title, _____'s *Family Story*. Help the child write her name on the cover of her book.

✳ Read the finished books together.

Extension Idea

Read the stories again. Ask, *Did you leave out any words? Do you want to add anything?*

Click on the *Between the Lions* website!

pbskids.org/lions/gryphonhouse

Video Clip: I Love My Family

CHAPTER 6

Feelings

This topic helps the children in your classroom learn to use language to name, understand, and express their feelings as they talk about what it means to feel afraid, sad, surprised, safe, and loved, as well as other emotions they feel when things don't go exactly as planned.

Feelings

Feelings come and feelings go,
Sometimes fast and sometimes slow.
Sometimes happy, sometimes sad,
Sometimes silly, sometimes mad.
Feelings come and feelings go,
Sometimes fast and sometimes slow.

Hunt for "Ff"

AGE 3+

Skill Focus
Fine Motor Skills
Letter Formation
Letter Recognition

Theme Connections
The Alphabet
Feelings

Vocabulary

clay	roll
curvy line	straight line
letter	trace
lowercase	uppercase

Materials
alphabet card
beads or buttons
blank large and small index
   cards
magnetic letters or alphabet
   blocks
marker

Preparation
- Write the uppercase and lowercase "Ff" on a large index card to create a letter "Ff" card. Display this card in the ABC Center.
- Write the uppercase and lowercase "Ff" on small index cards to create letter "Ff" cards for children to use in the ABC Center.
- Hide a few magnetic letters (or alphabet blocks) of the letter "Ff" in the ABC Center and throughout the classroom.

What to Do

✳ Select one letter of the alphabet. Focus on a letter that relates to feelings, a book you are reading to the children, or something that is happening in the classroom. In this case, the letter "Ff" (for feelings) is the example.

✳ Using a small letter "Ff" index card, trace over the straight lines on the uppercase "F" and the straight and curvy lines on the lowercase "f" to show the children how to form the letters.

✳ Have the children trace over the letters on the small letter "Ff" cards with their fingers and then place beads or buttons along the lines of the letters.

✳ Let the children go on a Letter Hunt in the ABC Center (and throughout the classroom if there are letters hidden throughout the classroom), searching high and low for hidden letters.

✳ When the children have found all the letters, ask them to hide them for the next group of children.

Click on the *Between the Lions* website!
pbskids.org/lions/gryphonhouse

Song: Library A to Z
Games: Theo's Puzzles (f)
       Sky Riding

Skill Focus

Compare and Contrast
Letter Recognition
Vocabulary

Theme Connections

The Alphabet
Feelings

Happy Fishing

AGE 3+

Preparation

- Make a fishing pole by attaching heavy string to the end of a yardstick or dowel. Tie a magnet to the other end of the string.
- Place several sets of magnetic letters "h," "a," "p," and "y," into a plastic tub (the "pond").
- Write the word *happy* on large index cards. Cut out pictures of happy-looking faces from magazines or catalogs and glue them on the word cards.

Vocabulary

arrange	lowercase
curvy line	match
first	shape
fish	straight line
letter	uppercase

Materials

fishing pole or string and
    yardstick or dowel
glue or tape
large index cards
magazines or catalogs
magnet
magnetic letters ("Hh," "Aa,"
    "Pp," and "Yy")
markers
plastic tub
scissors

What to Do

- Hold up the word card and read the word *happy*.
- Help the children identify and describe the shapes of the letter in the word *happy*.
- Have buddies help each other fish for the letters in *happy*.
- Encourage the children to talk about the shape of each letter pulled from the "pond" and then match the plastic letters to letters on the word card.

Extension Idea

Create more word cards that describe feelings, such as sad, angry, mad, shy, brave, tired, or surprised, and place the letters that spell those words in the tub "pond." Challenge the children to fish for the letters in these words and arrange the letters on the cards to make the words.

Click on the *Between the Lions* website!
pbskids.org/lions/gryphonhouse

Story: The Big Fish   **Poem:** Fish
Song: Upper and Lowercase   **Game:** Monkey Match

AGE 3+

Paint to Music

Skill Focus
Creative Expression
Fine Motor Skills
Vocabulary to Express Emotions

Theme Connections
Colors
Feelings
Music | Shapes

Vocabulary
calm	loud
energetic	peaceful
excited	quiet
fast	sad
feelings	slow
happy	soft

Materials
classical, rock, or other types of
   slow and fast music
fingerpaint
fingerpaint paper
music player

Preparation
• Cover work tables with newspaper or craft paper.
• Mix several colors of fingerpaint and place them in the Art Center.

What to Do
* Give the children large pieces of paper with spoonfuls of fingerpaint placed in the centers. Play soft, slow music. As the music plays, invite the children to fingerpaint to it.
* Model the activity as you move your fingers and hands to the rhythms and tempos of the music. Say, *I am moving my hands slowly. I am making a large, fluffy cloud. It makes me feel happy.*
* Then have the children listen to a fast, loud piece of music. Encourage them to move the paint on their papers to match the music.
* Ask the children how they feel as they listen to each piece of music.

Extension Idea
Encourage the children to discuss what is different about the two paintings they created, including the colors, the shapes, and the feelings they evoke.

Click on the *Between the Lions* website!
pbskids.org/lions/gryphonhouse
Stories: Elephants Can Paint Too!
           Yesterday I Had the Blues
Poem: Fingerpaints

Skill Focus

Fine Motor Skills

Creative Expression

Social and Emotional Skills

Theme Connections

Celebrations

Feelings

ART CENTER
Birthday Hats

AGE **3+**

Preparation

• Make a cone-shaped hat for each child—Cut out large paper circles. Cut a line from the outside edge to the center of each circle. Roll one of the cut edges over the other to form a cone and staple.

Vocabulary

birthday	hat
celebration	parade
excited	party
feelings	surprised
happy	traditions

What to Do

❋ Talk about birthdays, letting the children tell the group in the Art Center about special activities and traditions associated with their birthdays. Explain that birthdays are special days to celebrate the day they were born. How do birthday celebrations make them feel? Were they excited? Surprised?

❋ Read aloud *Bunny Cakes*.

❋ Let the children decorate party hats to wear to a birthday party.

❋ The children may want to glue feathers, sequins, lace, buttons, artificial flowers, or beads onto their hats. Some may glue fabric, yarn, or ribbon around the bottom or glue crepe paper strips to the top. Encourage creativity and the use of a variety of materials!

Materials

art scraps (feathers, sequins, lace, buttons, artificial flowers, beads, fabric, yarn, ribbon, crepe paper)

Bunny Cakes by Rosemary Wells or another book about birthdays (See page 219 for suggestions.)

glue

heavy paper

stapler

Extension Idea

Have the children sing "Happy Birthday" as they parade around the room in their birthday hats.

Click on the *Between the Lions* website!
pbskids.org/lions/gryphonhouse

Story: Happy Birthday, Cow!
Video Clips: Happy Birthday, Cliff Hanger!
           Dinos Read: celebrate

AGE 4+

Where's the Dog?

Skill Focus
Expressing Feelings
Hand-Eye Coordination
Vocabulary (Positional Words)

Theme Connections
Animals
Feelings
Homes and Houses

Vocabulary
behind   inside
beside   lost
doghouse   outside
in front of   sad

Materials
blocks
pencils
plastic or stuffed dogs
sticky notes

What to Do

✳ Have the children build a doghouse out of blocks for a stuffed or plastic dog. Encourage the children to write the dog's name on a sticky note and put it on the doghouse.

✳ To expand this experience, talk with the children as they engage in dramatic play, moving the dogs inside and outside the doghouse. Ask, *What's your dog's name? Where is the dog now? Is it inside (outside, in front of) the doghouse?*

✳ Invite the children to pretend that their dog gets out of the doghouse and is lost. Ask them to share how they feel and where they will look for their dog.

Extension Idea

Add a variety of building materials to the Blocks Center, including cardboard blocks, connecting cubes, unit blocks, hollow blocks, shaped blocks, alphabet blocks, magnetic-fit blocks, and bristle blocks, and suggest that the children build homes for other animals, such as horses, pigs, and birds.

Click on the *Between the Lions* website!
pbskids.org/lions/gryphonhouse

Story: How to Be a Good Dog
Poem: Doggy Days
Video Clip: Doghouse: near and far

Skill Focus

Hand-Eye Coordination

Identifying Feelings

Theme Connections

All About Me

Colors

Feelings

Shapes

BLOCK CENTER

Build a Cake

AGE 4+

What to Do

* Talk with the children about how they feel about celebrating special occasions by eating cake.
* Show pictures of many different cakes—birthday cakes, wedding cakes, cakes to celebrate the Fourth of July or other holidays.
* Have the children tell about their favorite cakes.
* Encourage the children to use the blocks to build cakes with many layers.
* Model how to stack the blocks to make your favorite cake—strawberry shortcake. Stack brown blocks to make a thick layer of cake. Stand red blocks on end for the strawberries. Balance flat white blocks on the next layer for whipped cream. And add a single red triangle to top off the cake.
* As the children finish their block cakes, encourage them to decorate the desserts with letters and other materials.

Vocabulary

balance   layers

build   levels

cake   stack

dessert   upright

flat

Materials

blocks of different colors, shapes, sizes

foam pieces

items to decorate a cake

pictures of cakes

plastic letters

Click on the *Between the Lions* website!

pbskids.org/lions/gryphonhouse

Stories: Edna Bakes Cookies

Happy Birthday, Cow!

LIBRARY CENTER

AGE 3+

Feelings Books

Skill Focus
Book Care and Handling
Choosing Books
Concepts of Print

Theme Connections
All About Me
Feelings

Vocabulary

author	grumpy
brave	illustration
care for	nosy
cover	predict
cross	shy
embarrassed	title
feelings	

Materials

fiction and nonfiction books about feelings (See page 221 for suggestions.)

Preparation

• Fill the Library Center with fiction and nonfiction books about feelings.

What to Do

✱ Encourage the children to select books that interest them and to look at the words and the pictures on their own or with another child.

✱ Model how to look at the illustrations on a book cover, predict what the book will be about, and decide whether you want to read it. Say, *This book has a picture of a little girl on the front, doing cartwheels and laughing. Myra, you love to do somersaults and cartwheels. And you always giggle and smile when you're doing them. You remind me of the girl in this story. Would you like to read this book?*

✱ Demonstrate how to hold, handle, and care for a book.

✱ Show the children where to begin reading and how to turn the pages.

✱ Encourage the children to look at the character's faces and describe how they might be feeling. Use the illustrations in the book to help the children understand the meaning of unfamiliar words such as *grumpy, nosy, embarrassed, cross, shy*, or *brave*.

Extension Idea

Suggest that the children retell their favorite book by "reading" the illustrations.

Click on the *Between the Lions* website!
pbskids.org/lions/gryphonhouse

Stories: Not Afraid of Dogs
Worm Watches
Song: Read a Book Today!

Skill Focus

Comprehension

Listening and Speaking

Retelling a Story

Theme Connections

Families

Feelings

Rocking-Chair Stories

AGE 4+

What to Do

✳ Read aloud *On Mother's Lap* to individuals or small groups in the Library Center.

✳ Sit in a rocking chair (if possible) and place in front of you two baby dolls, a toy boat, a blanket, and a stuffed dog.

✳ As you read, ask one child to play the role of Michael and add these items to your lap.

✳ Encourage all the children to make personal connections to the book. Ask, *Do you like to sit on your mother's (grandmother's, aunt's) lap? How do you feel? Would you want your brother, sister, or cousin to sit with you? Why or why not?*

✳ After reading the book, encourage the children to act out the story using the props.

Extension Idea

Encourage the children to look at and "read" other books about families (see suggestions on page 220).

Vocabulary

brother   sister

jealous   snuggle

safe   warm

Materials

baby dolls

blanket

crayons

drawing paper

On Mother's Lap by Ann Herbert Scott

rocking chair

stuffed dog

toy boat

Click on the *Between the Lions* website!

pbskids.org/lions/gryphonhouse

Story: My Dog Is as Smelly as Dirty Socks

AGE 4+

Count the Chips

Skill Focus

Counting

One-to-One Correspondence

Vocabulary

Theme Connections

Feelings

Food

Vocabulary

count	numbers
feelings	(1–10)
happy	shout
how many	stomp
match	

Materials

brown buttons

number chart

plastic dishes

red marbles

white playdough or clay

Note: You may want to focus on one number each day. For the children who are able, extend the activity to include numbers to nine or higher.

Preparation

- Make a Number Chart. Write the numbers from 1 to 5. Below each number, draw the corresponding number of dots. Post the chart in the Math and Science Center.
- Place white modeling playdough or clay ("vanilla ice cream"), brown buttons ("chocolate chips"), and red marbles ("cherries") in the Math and Science Center.

Safety note: Because this activity uses materials that pose a choking hazard (marbles and buttons), be sure to supervise the children's use of these materials.

What to Do

* Sing this song and do the motions.

If You're Happy and You Know It

If you're happy and you know it, clap your hands. (*Clap twice.*)
If you're happy and you know it, clap your hands. (*Clap twice.*)
If you're happy and you know it, then your face will surely show it. (*Point to face.*)
If you're happy and you know it, clap your hands. (*Clap twice.*)

2nd verse: Stomp your feet (*Stomp feet.*)
3rd verse: Shout "Hurray!" (*Shout "Hurray!"*)
4th verse: Do all three (*Clap twice, stomp feet, shout "Hurray!"*)

* Invite the children to talk about what makes them happy. Explain that eating ice cream makes you happy. Ask, *Does anyone else like ice cream? What is your favorite kind?*

* Suggest that the children place up to five chocolate chips (brown buttons) and up to five cherries (red marbles) on a scoop of vanilla ice cream (white playdough).

* Have the children use the Number Chart to count the number of chips by matching the chips to the number of dots and the numbers on the Number Chart. If necessary, model this process for the children.

Skill Focus

Cooperation

Expressing Feelings

Gross Motor Skills

Theme Connections

All About Me

Feelings

Quiet-Down Ball

AGE 3+

What to Do

- Share books that you've read about feelings, particularly those where a character feels angry. Ask, *Do you remember times when people in a book were angry? What happened?*
- Begin a discussion about how it feels to lose your temper and some things that you can do to calm down (time-out, get a hug, listen to soft music, talk it out, play a quiet game).
- Invite the children to play a game called Quiet-Down Ball. Have them sit in a circle with their legs apart and their feet touching the child's on each side of them. One child rolls an inflated beach ball to someone else in the circle. Play continues as the children roll the ball back and forth to one another.

Extension Idea

To make the game more fun, the children can use more than one beach ball.

Vocabulary

angry	quiet
calm	temper
feelings	time-out
hug	

Materials

inflated beach balls

Click on the Between the Lions website!

pbskids.org/lions/gryphonhouse

Story: Yesterday I Had the Blues

Monstrously Mad

Skill Focus
Exploring Magnets
Expressing Emotions
Vocabulary

Theme Connections
All About Me
Feelings

Vocabulary
bombaloo	magnet
emotions	monster
feelings	sad
happy	scrunch
mad	temper

Materials
glue

magnets (small magnets and
   horseshoe magnets)

markers

small index cards or pieces of
   card stock

Sometimes I'm Bombaloo by
   Rachel Vail or another book
   about feelings (See page
   221 for suggestions.)

Preparation
- Make magnetic monster faces by drawing mad monster faces on small index cards or pieces of card stock. See examples in the book *Sometimes I'm Bombaloo.*
- Glue a small magnet onto the back of each picture.

What to Do
✳ Read the book *Sometimes I'm Bombaloo* or another book about feelings. Lead a discussion about feelings and how Katie loses her temper. When Katie is mad, she becomes Bombaloo. She uses her feet and her fists instead of words and her face scrunches like a monster's.

✳ Hide the magnetic monster faces (see Preparation) in the sand. Let the children find the faces using large horseshoe magnets. As they unearth each monster face, invite them to mimic the mad monster faces they see.

✳ The children can also draw faces in the sand. Invite them to draw faces that show a range of emotions from happy to sad to monstrously mad.

Extension Idea
Practice writing skills by having the children write the words *sad* or *mad* in the sand. for children who need an extra challenge, suggest that they write the word *Bombaloo* in the sand. Place a copy of the book near the sand table to encourage this activity.

Click on the Between the Lions website!
pbskids.org/lions/gryphonhouse

Story: Yesterday I Had the Blues

Skill Focus

Curiosity

Fine Motor Skills

Theme Connections

Animals

Celebrations

Feelings

It's a Surprise!

AGE 3+

What to Do

- ⊠ Read the book *Bunny Cakes*. Remind the children that Max wants to make something special for Grandma Rabbit's birthday. What he makes will surprise her all right! Look back at the illustrations to see Max's earthworm cake.
- ⊠ Talk about what Max used to make and decorate his earthworm cake. Ask, *How do you think Grandma felt when she bit into a worm or a caterpillar?*
- ⊠ The children can use their hands and the molds to make earthworm cakes at the Sand Table. Encourage them to use the provided materials to decorate the cakes.

Extension Idea

Make lists of the ingredients in the earthworm cakes. The children can write and draw their lists, just like Max did in the story.

Vocabulary

cake	earthworm
caterpillar	icing
decorate	molds
decoration	tiers

Materials

Bunny Cakes by Rosemary Wells

cake or sand molds

pegs to use for candles

rubber worms and caterpillars

sand

sand table

shells

small rocks

Click on the Between the Lions website!

pbskids.org/lions/gryphonhouse

Story: Happy Birthday, Cow!

Video Clip: Opposite Bunny: yucky/yummy

Letter Molds ("Gg")

AGE 4+

Skill Focus
Fine Motor Skills

Letter Recognition

Theme Connections
The Alphabet

Feelings

Vocabulary

curvy	lowercase
first	mold
glad	sand
grumpy	straight
letter	trace
line	uppercase

Materials

index cards

plastic letter molds

sand

sand table

Preparation

• Write the uppercase and lowercase "Gg" on an index card to create a letter "Gg" card.

• Draw or cut out and paste a picture of a smiling face or a frowning face on an index card. Write the word *glad* or the word *grumpy* below the picture to create a word card for glad or grumpy.

What to Do

✳ Select one letter of the alphabet. Focus on a letter that relates to a feeling or emotion that you have learned about. In this case, the letter "Gg" (for glad or grumpy) is the example.

✳ Display the letter "Gg" card and trace over the straight and curvy lines to show how the letters are formed.

✳ Encourage the children to write an uppercase "G" and a lowercase "g" in the sand.

✳ Then have the children press molds for the letters "G" and "g" into the sand to make raised letters. Have them trace the letters with their fingers.

✳ Say, *You made the letter "Gg"! It's the first letter in the word* glad (or grumpy). Have the children point out the "g" on the word card for *glad.*

✳ Add new letter cards, word cards, pictures, and letter molds to the center. You might use:

"Ss" *surprised*	"Ee" *excited*	"Tt" *tired*	"Mm" *mad*
"Cc" *curious*	"Ww" *worried*	"hh" *happy*	"Ss" *sad*

Click on the *Between the Lions* website!

pbskids.org/lions/gryphonhouse

Story: Worm Watches

Song: The Two Sounds Made by g

Skill Focus

Concepts of Print (Functions of Print, Print Conveys Meaning)

Early Writing

Theme Connections

Feelings

Opposites (Front and Back)

WRITING CENTER
Greeting Card

AGE **4+**

What to Do

✳ Share a collection of greeting cards. Point out the front, inside, and the back of the cards. Talk about the words and pictures on each of the cards. You might say, *This card is for someone who is sick. Look at the balloons on the front. Balloons make people smile. The message on the inside says "I hope you feel better! Love, Emilio."*

✳ Give each child a folded piece of paper. Invite the children to draw a card for someone special and write their name on the inside.

✳ Act as a scribe and write the child's message on the card. As you write, talk about the letters and the spaces you leave between words. Point to the words as you read them aloud.

Vocabulary

back	front
card	inside
dear	love
deliver	message
from	

Materials

crayons

drawing paper

greeting cards

markers

Extension Idea

Talk with the children about how they will deliver their cards.

Click on the *Between the Lions* website!
pbskids.org/lions/gryphonhouse

Song: Got a Good Reason to Write

WRITING CENTER

Riddles About Me

Skill Focus
Concepts of Print (Print Conveys Meaning)
Early Writing

Theme Connections
All About Me
Feelings

Vocabulary

animal
clues
color
favorite

food
label
riddle
square

Materials

ball
crayons
paper squares

What to Do

✳ Ask the children to think about their favorite things. Name a category, such as food. Toss a ball to different children, and ask them to name their favorite food. Continue with favorite animals and colors.

✳ Help the children make picture cards about the things they like. Give each child four squares of paper. Have them draw pictures of their favorite food, animal, and color on three of the squares. On the fourth square, each child can write the first letter of his name.

✳ Help the children label the pictures and post them on a bulletin board. For example, if the child's name is Pedro and he likes hotdogs, hamsters, and the color blue, his squares would look like this:

Card #1: Picture of a hotdog, and the word "hotdog"
Card #2: Picture of a hamster, and the word "hamster"
Card #3: Something blue, and the word "blue"
Card #4: The letter "Pp"

✳ Make up a riddle about each child, using the clues on the board. Can the children guess who the riddle is about?
My favorite food is spaghetti.
My favorite animal is a hamster.
My favorite color is blue.
My name starts with the letter P.
Who am I?

Click on the *Between the Lions* website!
pbskids.org/lions/gryphonhouse

Story: My Dog Is as Smelly as Dirty Socks

CHAPTER 7

Food

With this topic, the children in your classroom learn about the foods that help their bodies grow strong. Fiction and nonfiction books about foods teach about many varieties of fruits and vegetables. Some adventurous characters encourage the children to try new foods. The children also begin to learn how to make their favorite foods and where we get food.

Mix a Pancake

Mix a pancake,
Beat a pancake,
Put it in a pan.
Cook a pancake,
Toss a pancake,
Catch it if you can.

AGE 3+

ABC CENTER

Food Letters

Skill Focus
Letter Recognition
Vocabulary

Theme Connections
The Alphabet
Food

Vocabulary

big	lowercase
find	search
food	small
letter	uppercase

Materials

advertisement flyers for food
glue sticks
magazines
marker
newspapers
scissors
three pieces of poster paper

Preparation

• Prepare three pieces of poster paper. Select three letters that are the beginning letters to words that are related to food. For example, start in alphabetical order with "Aa" for apple, "Bb" for beans, and "Cc" for carrots, or select three foods that are meaningful to the children and begin with those. For example, you might select "Mm" for macaroni, "Pp" for potato, and "Rr" for rice. This activity uses "Aa," "Bb," and "Cc."

• Write one letter on each piece of poster paper. On each piece of paper, glue a picture of a food that begins with that letter

What to Do

❋ Show the children the three pieces of poster paper.

❋ Have the children search through food flyers and ads in magazines and newspapers and cut out the letters "Aa," "Bb," and "Cc" that they find.

❋ If necessary, help the children paste the letters on the appropriate poster. Look at and talk about the completed posters together.

Extension Idea

Suggest that the children find pictures of food beginning with the focus letters and glue them to the pieces of poster board.

Click on the *Between the Lions* website!
pbskids.org/lions/gryphonhouse
Game: Sky Riding

Skill Focus

Creative Expression
Fine Motor Skills
Letter Recognition
Vocabulary

Theme Connections

The Alphabet
Food

Decorate Letter "Tt"

AGE 3+

Preparation

- Draw very large outlines of uppercase "T" and lowercase "t" on multiple sheets of paper.
- Create enough outlines for each child to have one uppercase letter "T" and one lowercase letter "t."

What to Do

※ Select one letter of the alphabet. Focus on a letter that relates to poems or stories you are reading about food. In this case, the letter "Tt" is used for *tomato*, *taco*, *turkey*, *toast*, *turnips*, and other foods that begin with "Tt."

※ Provide papers that have outlines of an uppercase "T" and lowercase "t" for every child.

※ Encourage the children to explore the shapes of the letters by tracing the outlines with their fingers.

※ Have the children use colored markers and crayons to decorate the letters with polka dots, stripes, squiggles, zigzags, and curly and wiggly lines.

※ Encourage them to talk about and describe the decorative marks they are making.

※ Suggest that the children draw a food beginning with "Tt" on their letters.

Vocabulary

curly	toast
decorate	tomato
dot	turkey
lines	turnips
polka dots	wiggly
stripes	zigzags
taco	

Materials

crayons and markers
scissors
white paper

Click on the *Between the Lions* website!
pbskids.org/lions/gryphonhouse

Stories: A Birthday for Cow!
Rabbit's Gift
Games: Theo's Puzzles (t)

ART CENTER
Tacos and Tamales

Skill Focus
Fine Motor Skills
Imaginative Play
Vocabulary

Theme Connections
Food
Shapes

Vocabulary

cheese
dough
fold
food
hot
husk
masa

meat
Mexican
roll
taco
tamale
vegetables

Materials

brown paper bags
modeling clay or playdough
    (brown, tan, red, green,
    yellow)
pictures of tacos and tamales
scissors

Preparation

- Post pictures of tacos and tamales in the Art Center.
- Cut brown paper bags into 6-inch diameter circles.

What to Do

✴ Say this rhyme together.

Yum, Yum, Yum
Tamales, tamales,
Yum, yum, yum.
Don't you wish you had some?
Taste so very, very yummy,
I wish I had some in my tummy.

✴ Explain that tamales are a kind of food from Mexico. Tamales have a soft dough, called *masa*, that is filled with meat, cheese, or vegetables. The tamale is rolled in a corn husk (outer covering of an ear of corn) and then cooked.

✴ The children can make tamales with modeling clay or playdough. Model this for them as you pretend to be a cook and demonstrate how to make a tamale. Say, *First, I will roll clay to make the flat masa. I will place the masa on a corn husk (paper bag circle). What should I put inside the tamale? I think I'll put meat in mine. Crumble up brown clay and put it on the tamale. Watch as I roll the tamale and pretend to cook it.*

✴ Encourage the children to make their own tamales with the materials.

Click on the *Between the Lions* website!
pbskids.org/lions/gryphonhouse

Story: Chicks and Salsa

Skill Focus

Creative Expression

Fine Motor Skills

Vocabulary

Theme Connections

Colors

Food

Shapes

ART CENTER

Fruit and Vegetable Faces

AGE 3+

Preparation

- Cut out pictures of food from grocery store flyers and glue them onto poster board to create a Food wall display. Sort the foods into two categories—fruits and vegetables. Post the chart in the Art Center.

What to Do

⊞ Look at the pictures on the Food wall display. Identify and talk about the different foods.

⊞ Have the children draw faces on paper plates. Encourage them to be very creative, using fruit and vegetable shapes and colors for the eyes, nose, hair, and mouth on their face. Spark their imaginations by saying, *A banana could make a funny nose. What other fruit or vegetables could we use for a nose? What could make a funny mouth?*

⊞ The children may enjoy looking at the book *Eating the Alphabet* to see what the illustrator/author Lois Ehlert used on her funny faces.

Extension Idea

Have the children write their names on index cards and display their artwork on a table.

Vocabulary

eye

frown

fruits (apple,
banana,
cherry,
grape,
orange,
and pear)

hair

mouth

nose

vegetables
(bean,
carrot,
corn, peas,
potato, and
squash)

Materials

crayons

Eating the Alphabet by Lois Ehlert or another book about fruits and/or vegetables (See page 223 for suggestions.)

glue

grocery store flyers

markers

paper plates

poster paper

scissors

Click on the *Between the Lions* website!
pbskids.org/lions/gryphonhouse

Song: Vegetable Medley

Poem: Otter's Picnic

Video Clip: Colorful Foods

BLOCK CENTER
Grocery Store

Skill Focus
Environmental Print
Imaginative Play
Sorting and Classifying

Theme Connections
The Alphabet
Colors
Food | My Community

Vocabulary

cans	grocery store
cash register	money
cost	pay
customer	price
dollars	shopping
fruit	shopping cart
groceries	vegetables

Materials

labeled empty food cans and
    cartons
large cardboard blocks
paper bags
pictures of food
play money
storage bins
toy cash register
toy food

Preparation
• Ask the children's families to send in clean, empty food cans and cartons from the grocery store. Check for any sharp edges.

What to Do

* Have the children build a pretend grocery store with the large cardboard blocks and bins. If they need prompting, ask them, *What do we need for the inside of our grocery store?* (toy food, shelves, cash register, shopping cart, and bags) Gather the materials and add them to the Block Center.

* As the children set up the inside of the store, encourage them to sort and organize the foods: fruits and vegetables on one shelf or in one bin, cans in another.

* The children can act out the roles of shoppers. Suggest that they look at and "read" the labels on the cans and boxes. Ask, *What is this? How do you know what's inside? Do you recognize any letters or words on this label?* Talk about how the pictures, colors, and letters help identify what is inside.

Extension Idea

Have the children write prices on the food items. As shoppers bring their items to the cash register, store clerks can collect money for the purchased items and bag them.

Skill Focus

Book Care and Handling

Choosing Books

Concepts of Print

Theme Connections

Colors

Farms

Food | My Community

Food Books

AGE 3+

Preparation

• Fill the Library Center with nonfiction books about food, restaurants, and grocery stores.

What to Do

✳ Encourage the children to select books that interest them and to look at the words and the pictures on their own or with another child.

✳ Model how to look at the illustrations on a book cover, predict what the book will be about, and decide whether you want to read it. Say, *This book has a picture of a farmer picking oranges from the top of a tree. We are having orange slices at snack time. Corey, did you ever wonder where oranges come from? You might like to read this book.*

✳ Demonstrate how to hold, handle, and care for a book.

✳ Show the children where to begin reading and how to turn the pages. Read parts of the book aloud. Pause to discuss the factual information in the book.

✳ Ask the children to describe the food featured in the book. Ask, *What color is it? Where does it grow (or how is it made)? Have you ever tasted this food? Would you like to?*

Extension Idea

Invite the children to draw a picture of a food from their favorite book.

Vocabulary

author	illustration
care for	predict
cover	taste
handle	title

Materials

crayons

drawing paper

nonfiction books about food (See page 222 for suggestions.), restaurants, and grocery stores (See page 225 for suggestions.)

Click on the *Between the Lions* website!
pbskids.org/lions/gryphonhouse

Stories: Bee-bim Bop!

Stone Soup

Stop That Pickle!

LIBRARY CENTER

AGE 3+

Food Favorites

Skill Focus
Book Appreciation
Choosing Books
Concepts of Print

Theme Connections
Folktales
Food

Vocabulary

carrot	predict
cover	soup
curious	title
illustration	trick
pattern	villager
potato	words

Materials

Stone Soup by Heather Forest or another fiction book about food that has predictable text

Preparation

• Fill the Library Center with fiction books about food. Include books with repeated and predictable text.

• Include several versions of well-known stories so the children can compare the illustrations and events.

What to Do

✳ Read aloud a book with predictable text, such as *Stone Soup*. Invite the children to participate in the reading by pretending to put ingredients into the soup and stirring the pot.

✳ After the pattern of the story has been established, pause to let the children predict what will happen as each curious villager inquires about the pot. You might say, *Can you spare a carrot for our soup?* Then pause to let the children look at the illustrations and tell what each villager will do.

✳ Encourage the children to "read" the book to find out how the soup turns out.

✳ Invite the children to select other books about food that interest them and to look at the words and the pictures on their own or with another child.

Extension Idea

Invite the children to draw a picture of the food that they like or a meal that they like to eat.

Click on the Between the Lions website!
pbskids.org/lions/gryphonhouse

Stories: Bee-bim Bop!
　　　　　Stone Soup
　　　　　Stop That Pickle!

Skill Focus
Counting

One-to-One Correspondence

Positional Words

Theme Connections
Families

Food

Shapes

MATH AND SCIENCE CENTER

Set the Table

AGE 3+

Preparation
- Make four to six paper placemats with an outline of each utensil, plate, cup, and napkin in its position.
- Put placemats for four to six place settings on a table.

What to Do

* Show the children how to set a table. Say, *Put the knives and spoons on the right side of each plate or bowl. Put the fork on the left side of the plate or bowl.*

* Tell the children there are three (four, five, or six) people coming to eat. Ask, *How many spoons (forks, knives, plates, glasses, napkins) do we need?* Have the children count out the items and then follow the outlines on the placemats to set the table.

Extension Ideas

* Explain that different families have different ways of setting a table. For example, show the children the cover of *Bee-bim Bop!* and observe how the little girl puts chopsticks and spoons next to each bowl to set the table.

* Have the children set the table using chopsticks in place of forks and knives.

Vocabulary

bowl	napkin
chopsticks	plate
fork	right
glass	set the table
knife	spoon
left	utensil

Materials
Bee-bim Bop! by Linda Sue Park (optional)

chopsticks (if unavailable, use two dowels or pencils)

large sheets of construction paper

napkins

paper or plastic glasses, bowls, and plates

plastic forks, knives, and spoons

Click on the Between the Lions website!
pbskids.org/lions/gryphonhouse

Story: Bee-bim Bop!

Fruit Sorter

Skill Focus

Compare and Contrast

Counting

Sorting and Classifying

Theme Connections

Colors

Food | Numbers

Opposites (Big and Small)

AGE 4+

Vocabulary

big

different

fruit (banana,
    grape,
    orange,
    pear, and
    so on)

green

grid

orange

red

same

small

sort

square

yellow

Materials

marker

masking tape

mural paper

plastic fruit

ruler

tape

Preparation

- On a piece of mural paper, make a grid with several 1-foot squares. Tape the grid to the floor.
- Write the numerals 1 to 5 on index cards. On each card, draw the corresponding number of dots. Make two sets of number cards for this activity.

What to Do

✳ Let the children use the floor grid to sort fruits. Model what to do by picking up an apple. Say, *This is an apple. I am going to place it in this square. Look, here's another apple. I am going to put it in the same square as the other apple. Here's a pear. It's not an apple. Let's put it in a new square. Can anyone find another pear to put in the pear square?*

✳ When the children have finished sorting, ask them to count the pieces of fruit in each square. You might say, *We have five apples and two pears!*

✳ Have them place a number card in each square to show how many pieces of fruit there are.

Extension Idea

Have the children sharpen their observation skills by describing the different shapes and colors of each type of fruit, such as, *This apple is big and red. This apple is small and green.*

Click on the *Between the Lions* website!

pbskids.org/lions/gryphonhouse

Story: Otter's Picnic

Video Clip: Colorful Foods

Skill Focus
Concepts of Print
Imaginative Play
Listening and Speaking

Theme Connections
Families
Food

Cooking in the Kitchen

AGE
3+

Preparation
- If you do not have child-sized appliances for the Pretend and Play Center, help the children make them from appliance boxes. Cut out doors and then draw knobs, burners, and door handles to make refrigerators, stoves, and microwave ovens.
- Label the appliances (stove, refrigerator, microwave).

What to Do

✳ Say this rhyme together, inviting the children to add motions for each line.

Mix a Pancake
Mix a pancake,
Beat a pancake,
Put it in a pan.
Cook a pancake,
Toss a pancake,
Catch it if you can.

✳ Invite the children to take turns role playing an adult and a child cooking pancakes and other meals together.

✳ While the children are cooking meals and experimenting with the different cooking utensils, clothing, and appliances, introduce them to different kitchen terms and vocabulary. For example, *You are using a* spatula *to flip the pancakes.* Or, *I see that you are washing the* skillets *when you finish cooking, and you are stacking them in the* dish drainer *to dry.*

Vocabulary
appliance	pan
apron	pancake
bake	refrigerator
beat	skillet
chop	spatula
cook	stove
microwave	toss
mix	

Materials
apron
bowls
plastic spoons
play stove
play refrigerator
pots and pans
spatula
toy food items

Click on the Between the Lions website!
pbskids.org/lions/gryphonhouse

Stories: Bee-bim Bop!
Chicks and Salsa
Making Bread

AGE 4+

Chopsticks

Skill Focus
Fine Motor Skills

Imaginative Play

Sharing Ideas

Theme Connections
Colors

Families

Food | Shapes

Vocabulary
bowl	fork
chopsticks	spoon
fingers	utensil

Materials
bowls

felt pieces

forks and spoons

chopsticks (if not available, substitute two pencils)

pompoms

scissors

tablecloth

Preparation
- Fill small bowls with felt cut into different shapes to resemble green beans, orange carrots, and blue fish. Use different colored pompoms for berries, peas, and cherry tomatoes.

What to Do

✳ Engage the children in a discussion about the utensils they use to eat. Hold up forks, spoons, and a set of chopsticks as examples. Explain that people use different types of utensils for eating. Some families use chopsticks for cooking and eating certain foods.

✳ Show the children how to hold chopsticks and to use them to pick up food. It may be easier for the children to manipulate the chopsticks if you rubber band them together near the top.

✳ Invite the children to pick up the pretend beans, carrots, fish, berries, peas, cherry tomatoes, and other foods with their chopsticks.

✳ Caution the children that this is not real food and should not be placed in their mouths.

✳ Offer a challenge by suggesting that the children move the pretend food from one bowl to another. An additional challenge would be to move specific amounts from one bowl to another. For example, the children could place one green bean, two carrots, three pieces of fish, four berries, five peas, and six cherry tomatoes into one bowl, or move them from one bowl to another.

Note: Place *Cleversticks* by Bernard Ashley in the Pretend and Play Center for children to look at and enjoy.

Skill Focus

Fine Motor Skills

Letter Recognition

Theme Connections

The Alphabet

Farms

Food

Letter Molds ("Ff," "Gg")

AGE 4+

Preparation

- Write the uppercase and lowercase "Ff" and "Gg" on index cards to create letter cards for "Ff" and "Gg."
- Draw or cut out and paste a picture of a farm on one index card and a little garden on another index cards. Write the word farm or garden below the pictures to create two word cards.

Vocabulary

curvy	mold
first	sand
letter	straight
line	trace
lowercase	uppercase

What to Do

- ✳ Select one letter of the alphabet. Focus on a letter that relates to food, especially places where food is grown. In this case, the letter "Gg" is the example. *Have any of the children ever had a garden? What did they grow in it?*
- ✳ Display the letter "Gg" card and trace over the curvy lines and then the straight lines to show how the letters are formed.
- ✳ Encourage the children to write uppercase "G" and lowercase "g" in the sand. Then have the children press molds for the letters "G" and "g" into the sand to make raised letters. Have them trace the letters with their fingers.
- ✳ Say, *You made the letter "g"! It's the first letter in the word* garden. Have the children point out the "g" on the word card.
- ✳ Add new letter cards for "Ff," a word card for *farm*, and pictures to the center.

Materials

index cards

pictures of a farm and a garden or markers

plastic letter molds

sand

sand table

Extension Idea

Help the children use letter molds to make the word *farm* in the sand. Provide the word card for them to match letters.

Click on the *Between the Lions* website!

pbskids.org/lions/gryphonhouse

Stories: Chicks and Salsa | The Little Red Hen

Song: The Two Sounds Made by g

Poem: You Never Hear the Garden Grow

Sand Cookies

Skill Focus
Counting

Measuring

Vocabulary

Theme Connections
Food

Imagination

Vocabulary

bake

chocolate
  chips

cup

egg

egg beater

flour

measure

milk

mix

sifter

spoon

sugar

Materials

chart paper

cookie sheets

egg beater

marker

measuring cups

measuring spoons

plastic eggs

sand

sand table

sifter

Preparation
• Pour some water into the sand to make it damp and easier to pack.

What to Do

✳ Tell the children that they are going to make pretend cookies.

✳ Brainstorm with the children a list of ingredients they might like to put in their cookies, such as flour, eggs, chocolate chips, walnuts, sugar, and so on.

✳ Write a pretend recipe using the ingredients that the children suggested, such as:

2 cups flour

1 cup sugar

1 cup chocolate chips

2 eggs

4 tablespoons walnuts

2 tablespoons milk

✳ Show the children how to measure sand, using cups and spoons.

✳ Let the children follow the pretend recipe to measure, scoop, mix, and spoon the sand to make cookies.

Extension Idea

Add sifters, eggbeaters, and other cooking utensils to the Sand Table, and let the children experiment with new, pretend recipes.

Click on the *Between the Lions* website!

pbskids.org/lions/gryphonhouse

Stories: Edna Bakes Cookies

Making Bread

Skill Focus
Concepts of Print
Early Writing
Writing Name

Theme Connections
All About Me
Colors
Food | Shapes

We Make Pizza

AGE 4+

Preparation
- Cut out large triangles (slices of pizza) from heavy paper.
- Write this sentence frame on each triangle:

  _____ puts _____ on pizza.

What to Do

⬛ Tell the children that you are going to create a book called "We Make Pizza." Each child will contribute a page to the book.

⬛ Brainstorm a list of toppings that they might like to put on their pizza, such as tomato sauce, mushrooms, cheese, pepperoni, ham, pineapple, bell peppers, ground beef, and so on.

⬛ Read the sentence frame together:
(Child's name) puts (toppings) on pizza.

⬛ Think aloud as you complete the sentence. *I will write my name on the first line. Mrs. Williams puts _____ on pizza. I like cheese pizza, so I will write* cheese *on the line.*

⬛ Point out the beginning and ending of each word and the spaces between the words.

⬛ Have the children complete the sentence on one of the pizza slices.

⬛ Ask each child to color the pizza slice, adding the topping she wrote about.

⬛ Compile the pages into a class book. Create a cover.

Extension Idea

Ask each child to read her page to the class or to you. Put the book in the Library Center for the children to read.

Vocabulary
bell peppers	pineapple
cheese	pizza
cover	sauce
create	sentence
ground beef	spaces
ham	toppings
mushrooms	triangle
pepperoni	write

Materials
crayons
heavy paper
markers
scissors
stapler

WRITING CENTER

Who Stole the Onions?

Skill Focus

Early Writing

Listening and Speaking

Early Writing

Theme Connections

Animals

Farms

Food

Vocabulary

barnyard	name
chant	salsa
chick	vegetable
farmer	word
garden	write
letters	

Materials

Chicks and Salsa by Aaron
   Reynolds

crayons

glue

heavy paper

scissors

wooden sticks

Preparation

• Cut 6-inch ovals from heavy paper.

What to Do

❋ Tell the children that they are going to write a new part for a chant and act it out.

❋ Explain that in a book called *Chicks and Salsa*, the barnyard animals get tired of their regular food and decide to fix some spicy Mexican food instead. The ingredients are stolen from the farmer's garden.

❋ Say the following chant together several times.

Who Stole the Onions from the Farmer's Yard?
Class: *Who stole the onions from the farmer's yard?*
Class: *The chickens stole the onions from the farmer's yard.*
Chickens: *Who me?*
Class: *Yes, you!*
Chickens: *Couldn't be!*
Class: *Then who?*

❋ Ask, *What other vegetables do you think should go into the salsa? Who will pick the vegetables?* Add these new vegetables to the chant so you have more verses

❋ Have the children use the ovals of paper to draw the farmyard animal holding the vegetable they've chosen.

❋ The children can glue the drawing onto a craft stick to make a puppet.

❋ Ask each child to write his name on the back of his puppet.

❋ On the front of the puppet, have him attempt to write the name of the animal using scribbles, letter-like symbols, letters, or the entire word.

CHAPTER 8

Friends

This topic focuses on all kinds of friendships, including the remarkable friendship between a baby hippo and an aging, giant tortoise. The story teaches the children in your classroom that they can be friends with anyone, no matter how different they think that person may be. The children also explore how to make friends and develop social skills as they play and learn together.

The More We Get Together

The more we get together,
Together, together,
The more we get together,
The happier we'll be.

ABC CENTER

Letter Shaping ("Bb")

Skill Focus
Fine Motor Skills
Letter Formation
Letter Recognition

Theme Connections
The Alphabet
Friends
Shapes

Vocabulary
buddy   shaving cream
curved   straight
shape

Materials
alphabet chart
blank index cards
markers
pipe cleaners
shaving cream
sponge

Preparation
• Write the uppercase and lowercase "Bb" on an index card to create a "Bb" letter card.

What to Do

✳ Select one letter of the alphabet. Focus on a letter that is the first letter in a word that relates to the topic *friends*. In this case, the letter "Bb" (for *buddy*) is the example.

✳ Display the letter "Bb" card. Use your finger to trace over both the uppercase and lowercase letter "Bb" on the card to show the children how to form the letters.

✳ Point out the straight lines and the curved lines on the letters. Have the children find objects in the classroom that have straight parts, such as blocks, paper, and books, and objects in the classroom that have curved parts, such as blocks, scissors, and balls.

✳ Show the children how to use pipe cleaners to form the letters "Bb."

✳ Invite the children to practice writing "Bb" with their fingers in the shaving cream.

Extension Idea

Have the children look for things in the classroom that go together (for example, sand and pail, drum and drumstick, and cars and trucks), just like buddies go together.

Click on the *Between the Lions* website!
pbskids.org/lions/gryphonhouse
Game: Theo's Puzzles (b)

Skill Focus
Fine Motor Skills
Letter Recognition
Vocabulary
Word Recognition

Theme Connections
The Alphabet
Friends

ABC CENTER

Fish for "y-e-s"

AGE 3+

Preparation
- Write *yes* on an index card to create a *yes* word card.
- Tie a magnet to one end of a string and tie the other end to a ruler or dowel to make a magnetic fishing pole.

What to Do
❋ Display the *yes* word card.
❋ Have the children repeat the word with you and identify the first letter: "Yy."
❋ Put the magnetic letters into a bucket or another container.
❋ Suggest that the children fish for the letters in *yes*, then arrange the letters to match the letters on the word card.

Extension Idea
Create other cards with words related to friendship (for example, *pal*, *help*, *friend*, and *together*) or the name of one of the children's friends. Have the children search for the letters in the words.

Vocabulary
first	middle
last	second
letter	third
magnet	word
match	

Materials
blank index card
bucket
magnet
markers
ruler or dowel
several sets of magnetic letters
    "y," "e," and "s"
string

Click on the *Between the Lions* website!
pbskids.org/lions/gryphonhouse

Story: Yo! Yes?
Game: Monkey Match

ART CENTER

Friend Sculptures

Skill Focus
Compare and Contrast
Creative Expression
Fine Motor Skills
Vocabulary

Theme Connections
Animals
Friends | Parts of the Body

Vocabulary

ears	round
face	shell
feet	short
friends	snout
head	thick
hippo	thin
hippopotamus	turtle
large	wide
mouth	

Materials

modeling clay

Owen & Mzee: Best Friends by Isabella Hatkoff or another book about friends (See pages 222–223 for suggestions.)

pictures of hippos and turtles

Preparation
- Post pictures of hippos and turtles on a chart.

What to Do

❊ Begin a discussion about friends, exploring the idea that two people can be friends even if they are very different from each other.

❊ Encourage the children to look at the pictures of the hippo and the turtle. Talk about the features of each animal. A hippo has a large round body, thick legs, big round ears, a big nose (snout), and a wide mouth. A turtle has a hard round shell, short legs, a thin neck, and a small face.

❊ In nature, hippos and turtles do not often have a chance to become friends. But in the book *Owen and Mzee*, the two animals become best buddies, eating, sleeping, and playing together.

❊ Have the children roll, pinch, press, or mold the clay to make turtles and hippos.

Extension Idea

The children can play with their clay hippos and turtles, making up stories about the things the two animals do together.

Click on the *Between the Lions* website!
pbskids.org/lions/gryphonhouse
Story: Owen and Mzee
Video Clip: If You Were: hippo

Skill Focus

Cooperation

Creative Expression

Fine Motor Skills

Theme Connections

All About Me

Friends

Parts of the Body

ART CENTER
Friendship Chain

AGE 4+

Preparation

- Cut pieces of bulletin-board paper into lengths that approximate the height of the children in your class.

What to Do

⊠ Explain that a *buddy* is someone you work closely with. She is your friend.

⊠ Tell the children that in this activity, buddies will take turns tracing each other on large sheets of paper.

⊠ Have one child lie on the paper with arms stretched out to her sides. Her buddy traces an outline of her body. Then the two switch roles.

⊠ Encourage the buddies to work together and use the materials to decorate the figures.

⊠ Cut out and hang the completed figures on a wall, side-by-side, with hands touching to make a friendship chain.

Extension Idea

Have the children write their names on their figures. Investigate to find names that begin with the same letter.

Vocabulary

body   share

buddy   take turns

friend   trace

outline

Materials

art scraps (small shapes cut from colored construction paper, cotton balls, feathers, glitter, ribbons, sequins, stickers, and yarn)

bulletin-board paper

crayons

glue

markers

Click on the *Between the Lions* website!

pbskids.org/lions/gryphonhouse

Story: Yo! Yes?

BLOCK CENTER

Team Towers

Skill Focus
Cooperation

Hand-Eye Coordination

Measuring

Theme Connections
Friends

Neighborhoods

Vocabulary

build	measure
compare	team
construct	teamwork
height	tower
high	

Materials
variety of blocks

digital camera, optional

What to Do

✳ Have two friends of different heights stand beside each other. Ask the children which of the friends is shorter and which is taller.

✳ Have two or three friends work together as a team to build the tallest tower they can before the blocks fall over.

Note: If possible, take pictures of the tower as the friends build it. Print the photographs and ask the friends to put them in sequence.

✳ When a team is done, encourage the members to describe their tower. Ask, *How did you build it? Why did it fall down?*

Extension Idea

Encourage the children to use one type of block (only square blocks, only red blocks, only Legos, and so on) to build towers. *How are these towers the same? How are they different?*

Click on the *Between the Lions* website!

pbskids.org/lions/gryphonhouse

Video Clip: Opposite Bunny: built/demolished, sad/happy

Skill Focus

Cooperative Play
Hand-Eye Coordination
Sorting and Classifying
Vocabulary

Theme Connections

Animals
Friends | Habitats

A Park for Animal Friends

AGE 4+

What to Do

✱ Invite the children to create a nature park using blocks. Explain that a nature park is a safe place for wild animals to live.

✱ Encourage the children to make closed-in spaces for different types of animals.

✱ Talk about what kind of habitat each animal needs. For example, because hippos like water, their space will need a pond. Monkeys like to swing from branches, so they need a space with trees.

✱ Encourage the children to sort the toy animals into groups. Ask, *Which animals are friends? Which animals do you want to put together?*

Vocabulary

habitat   nature park
hippo   pond
land   trees
leaves   water
monkey

Materials

blocks
markers
paper
small plastic animals

Extension Idea

Help the children make labels and name cards for the different animals and habitats.

Click on the *Between the Lions* website!
pbskids.org/lions/gryphonhouse

Story: Owen and Mzee

LIBRARY CENTER

Yo, Friend!

Skill Focus
Book Handling
Identifying Feelings
Story Comprehension
Vocabulary

Theme Connections
Feelings
Friends

Vocabulary
excited	happy
expression	lonely
face	sad
friends	shy
hands	

Materials
crayons
drawing paper
fiction books about friends and
    friendships (See pages
    222–223 for suggestions)
Yo! Yes? by Chris Raschka

Preparation
• Fill the Library Center with fiction books about friends and
friendships.

What to Do

✴ Show the cover of the book *Yo! Yes?* Explain that the story is
about two lonely boys. Say, *I wonder if the boys will become
friends. Let's read the story to find out.* Read aloud *Yo! Yes?* to the
children.

✴ Show the children where to begin reading and how to turn the
pages. As you read, say, *Look at the boy's face. Look at his body.*
Ask, *What do you think he is feeling? What could he be thinking?*

✴ Invite the children to select other books about friends that
interest them and to look at the words and the pictures on their
own or with another child.

✴ Ask them to use the illustrations to discover what the friends do
together and to look at their faces to see how they feel.

Extension Idea
Who would the children like to be friends with in the books? Have
them draw pictures of these characters.

Click on the *Between the Lions* website!
pbskids.org/lions/gryphonhouse

Stories: The Lion and the Mouse
            Violet's Music
            Yo! Yes?

Skill Focus
Book Care and Handling
Choosing Books
Concepts of Print

Theme Connections
Feelings
Friends

Books About Friends

AGE 3+

Preparation
• Fill the Library Center with nonfiction books about friends and different kinds of friendships.

What to Do

☒ Encourage the children to select books that interest them and to look at the words and the pictures on their own or with a buddy.

☒ Model how to look at the illustrations on a book cover, predict what the book will be about, and decide whether you want to read it. Say, *The cover of this book has a picture of two girls holding teddy bears. You like teddy bears. You might like to read this book.*

☒ Demonstrate how to hold, handle, and care for a book.

☒ Show the children where to begin reading and how to turn the pages. Read parts of the book aloud. Pause to discuss what is happening in the book.

☒ Use the illustrations in the book to help the children understand how the friends feel. Draw attention to the expressions on the characters' faces. Ask, *How do you think this friend feels? How can you tell? What do you think happened to make the friend feel this way?*

Vocabulary
author
cover
expression
friends

handle
illustration
predict
title

Materials
books about friends and
  different kinds of friendships
  (See pages 222–223 for
  suggestions.)

Click on the Between the Lions website!
pbskids.org/lions/gryphonhouse

Story: Owen and Mzee

MATH AND SCIENCE CENTER

Buddy Math

Skill Focus
Collecting Data
Counting
Name Recognition

Theme Connections
Counting
Friends

Vocabulary
buddy   grid
compare   letters
count   name
friends   together

Materials
markers
name cards
plastic letters
strips of paper

Preparation
- Draw a grid with 10 boxes (or more) in each of two rows.

What to Do

✳ Brainstorm pairs of friends that are familiar to the children, such as Owen and Mzee, Lionel and Leona, Frog and Toad, and the lion and the mouse.

✳ Write the words *Lionel* and *Leona* on separate strips of paper. Let the children find the plastic letters to match the letters in the words.

✳ Model how to put the letters on the grid, with one letter in each space. Put one name from the pair of friends on one line, and the other name on the other line.

L	i	o	n	e	l				
L	e	o	n	a					

✳ Have the children determine which name has the most letters, which one has fewer, or if the names have the same number of letters. The children can also count how many letters there are in both names.

✳ Have two buddies put their own names on the grid to show that they are friends.

Click on the *Between The Lions* website!

pbskids.org/lions/gryphonhouse

Stories: The Lion and the Mouse
Owen and Mzee
Yo! Yes?

Skill Focus

Predicting

Sorting and Comparing

Vocabulary

Theme Connections

Friends

Opposites (Tall and Short, Loud
and Quiet)

Which One Is Heavy?

AGE 4+

What to Do

* Think of friends who are opposites. Maybe one is short and one is tall, one is hungry while one is full, or one is loud and the other is quiet. Friends may be different weights too—one heavy and one light.

* Demonstrate how to weigh objects on a balance scale. Place a big ball of clay in one hand and a small ball of clay in the other. Show how you examine the clay balls and guess which is heavier and which is lighter.

* Place the clay balls on the balance scale. Ask the children to describe what they see. Explain that the heavier object will make that side of the scale go down. The lighter object will go up.

* Put out a box of objects. The children can explore weight by picking two objects at a time, observing them, and making predictions about which one is heavier and which is lighter.

* After the children have guessed, let them test the objects on the scale to see if their predictions were correct.

Vocabulary

balance scale   lighter

heavier   weigh

heavy   weight

Materials

balance scale

clay

objects of varying weights
    (blocks, books, feathers,
    plastic animals, and so on)

Extension Idea

Challenge the children by having them compare three objects. After they weigh two of the objects, they can take the heavier object and compare it to the third one. Which of the three is the heaviest?

PRETEND AND PLAY CENTER

New Friends

Skill Focus
Cooperation
Imaginative Play
Listening and Speaking

Theme Connections
Friends
Homes and Houses

Vocabulary
buddy
decorate
door
friend
home
share
take turns
window

Materials
large appliance box
markers
paint
paintbrushes
scissors
stuffed animals
writing materials

Preparation
- Cut a door and window into a large appliance box to make a cardboard home.
- Fill the home with stuffed animals and other soft toys.

What to Do

✳ Invite the children to decorate the cardboard home with paint or markers.

✳ Pair children up, and have the buddies pretend that they are new friends.

✳ Model words and actions that might be used when you meet someone for the first time. Say, *Hi!* (wave) *My name is Antonio.* (smile) *What's your name?* (look at person) *Would you like to play with my stuffed animals?*

✳ The children should take turns inviting their new friend to play in their home. Encourage them to take turns and share toys with their new friend and explore new things they can play together.

Extension Idea

On an other day, add writing materials to the Pretend and Play Center. Encourage the children to use them to write their names, draw pictures, or play tic-tac-toe.

Click on the *Between the Lions* website!
pbskids.org/lions/gryphonhouse

Story: Yo! Yes?

Skill Focus
Creative Movement
Imaginative Play
Listening to Music
Vocabulary

Theme Connections
Friends
Music

Dance Stage

AGE 3+

What to Do

* Pair the children up and invite each pair of buddies to present a short dance.
* Before they begin, remind the children that buddies work together, helping each other, and saying things to make each other feel good.
* Introduce and demonstrate dance movements, such as tapping your foot, kicking your leg in the air, jumping, marching, and any other movement that is fun and easy for the children to do.
* Let buddies put on costumes and dance together. At the end of the dance, the dancers can take a bow.
* Encourage the other children in the learning center to applaud for the dancers and respond with positive comments such as, *You are a good dancer.* Or *I like the way you walked on your tiptoes.*

Vocabulary

applaud	slide
bend	tap
bow	tiptoe
dance	turn
dancer	twirl
partner	

Materials
costumes and props (capes, tutus, scarves, ribbons)
dance music and a music player

Extension Idea
Take photos of the children dancing and post them on a bulletin board. Have the children write their name under their pictures.

Click on the *Between the Lions* website!
pbskids.org/lions/gryphonhouse

Song: Dance in Smarty Pants

Sand Duet

Skill Focus
Cooperation
Experiment with Instruments
Fine Motor Skills

Theme Connections
Friends
Music

AGE 3+

Vocabulary

dance
friends
gold
jar
lid

rhythm
sand
shaker
silver
soft

Materials

sand
sand table
scoops
spoons
unbreakable jars with lids

Note: If you are unfamiliar with this song or any other song in this book, use a search engine to find places on the web where you can hear it.

Preparation

- Place small non-breakable jars with their lids in the Sand Table. Add scoops and spoons.

What to Do

✳ Tell the children that they are going to make sand shakers and play them with some friends.

✳ Have each child put a small amount of sand into a jar and put the lid back on. Be sure the lids are on tight.

✳ Have the children select a song about friends to sing together, such as "Make New Friends." As they sing, the children shake their shakers and dance to the rhythm of the music.

Make New Friends
Make new friends,
But keep the old.
One is silver,
The other is gold.

A circle is round,
It has no end.
That's how long,
I will be your friend.

You have one hand,
I have the other.
Put them together, (children hold hands)
We have each other.

Click on the Between the Lions website!
pbskids.org/lions/gryphonhouse

Story: Violet's Music
Video Clip: Fred: Musical Instruments
Game: Dub Cubs

Skill Focus

Fine Motor Skills

Letter Recognition

Theme Connections

The Alphabet

Friends

SAND TABLE CENTER

Letter Molds ("Dd")

AGE 4+

Preparation

- Write the uppercase and lowercase "Dd" on an index card to create letter card "Dd."
- Draw or cut out and paste a picture of a child dancing on an index card. Write the word *dance* below the picture to create a word card for dance.

Vocabulary

first	sand
letter	straight
line	trace
lowercase	uppercase
mold	

Materials

index cards

picture of child dancing

plastic letter molds

sand

sand table

What to Do

- ✖ Select one letter of the alphabet. Focus on a letter that relates to friends or friendship. In this case, the letter "Dd" is the example for dancing, something you can do with a friend.
- ✖ Display the letter "Dd" card and trace over the curvy lines and the straight lines to show how the letters are formed.
- ✖ Encourage the children to write uppercase "D" and lowercase "d" in the sand. Then have the children press molds for the letters "D" and "d" into the sand to make raised letters. Have them trace the letters with their fingers.
- ✖ Say, *You made the letter "d"! It's the first letter in the word* dance. Have the children point out the "d" on the word card.
- ✖ Add new letter cards and word cards to the center, such as:
  "Bb" buddy
  "Hh" hug
  "Ff" friend

Click on the Between the Lions website!
pbskids.org/lions/gryphonhouse

Song: Dixie Chimps: Delighted You're Mine
Video Clip: Dance in Smarty Pants
Game: Theo's Puzzles (d)

Buddy Notes

AGE 4+

Skill Focus

Concepts of Print (Functions of Print, Print Conveys Meaning)

Early Writing

Social and Emotional Awareness

Vocabulary

Theme Connections

Feelings | Friends

Vocabulary

deliver	note
fold	splendid
friend	super
marvelous	wonderful

Materials

class name chart

crayons

drawing and writing paper

markers

A Splendid Friend, Indeed by
Suzanne Bloom

Preparation

- Make a class name chart. If possible, take a photo of each child, and put it beside the name on the chart.

What to Do

✳ Read aloud the book, *A Splendid Friend, Indeed.*

✳ Remind the children of the note Goose wrote to Bear in the story. The note said "I like you. Indeed I do. You are my splendid friend." Explain that *splendid* means *super, marvelous,* or *wonderful.*

✳ Have each child write a short note to a buddy. Suggest that they tell their buddies something they like to do together. The children can draw and scribble or attempt to write letters.

✳ The children can fold their notes and write their buddy's name on the front. Provide name cards for the children to copy.

Extension Idea

Arrange a time for buddies to deliver and read their notes to each other.

Click on the *Between the Lions* website!

pbskids.org/lions/gryphonhouse

Story: Yo! Yes?

Songs: Fabulous

Got a Good Reason to Write

Homes and Houses

The children in your classroom will learn more about themselves and their families by exploring homes and houses—a source of warmth, love, and security. As they compare and contrast different kinds of houses and building materials, they begin to develop an understanding of cause-and-effect relationships and of similarities and differences. The children will also develop an awareness of the natural world as they learn about animal homes and habitats.

Here Is the Beehive

Here is the beehive,
But where are the bees?
Living inside where nobody sees.
Soon they come flying out of the hive,
One! Two! Three! Four! Five!
Very awake and very alive!
Six! Seven! Eight! Nine! Ten!
Then they fly back in again.

AGE 3+

ABC CENTER
Hunt for h-o-m-e

Skill Focus
Alphabet Awareness
Letter Recognition

Theme Connections
The Alphabet
Homes and Houses

Vocabulary

alphabet	home
begins	house
chart	hunt
disappear	letter
find	lost

Materials

index cards
marker
wooden alphabet blocks or
 plastic letters

Preparation

• Before the children arrive, hide the letters "Hh," "Oo," "Mm," and "Ee" in the ABC Center or around the classroom. Use wooden alphabet blocks or plastic letters.
• Write *home* (or *HOME* if the hidden letters are uppercase letters) on an index card.

What to Do

✳ Explain to the children that a strange thing has happened. You had some letters on the table this morning and some of them have disappeared.

✳ Point to the *home* word card, and ask the children to identify the letters. These are the letters that are lost.

✳ Ask the children to go on a hunt to find the lost letters. When a child finds a letter, she covers that letter on the home word card.

Extension Ideas

Suggest that the children draw pictures of their homes or places they would like to live.

Click on the *Between the Lions* website!
pbskids.org/lions/gryphonhouse

Story: Beeper Paints
Song: My House

Skill Focus
Alphabet Awareness

Letter Recognition

Theme Connections
The Alphabet

Animals

Homes and Houses

"Hh" Is for Homes and Houses

AGE 3+

Preparation
- Draw very large outlines of uppercase "H" and lowercase "h" on multiple sheets of paper. Cut enough for each child to have one uppercase letter "H" and one lowercase letter "h."

What to Do
- ✳ Say the word *house*, emphasizing the beginning sound. Tell the children that the word *house* begins with the letter "Hh."
- ✳ Provide a paper uppercase "H," and a lowercase "h" for each child.
- ✳ Encourage the children to explore the shapes of the letters by tracing the outlines with their fingers.
- ✳ Give the children magazines, newspapers, and catalogs that have pictures of houses and homes in them.
- ✳ The children can cut out pictures of houses and homes and glue them onto the uppercase "H" and lowercase "h."

Extension Idea
Use masking tape to create an uppercase "H" on the floor. Encourage the children to walk along the straight lines of the letter.

Vocabulary
home

house

lowercase

shape

uppercase

Materials
construction paper

crayons

glue sticks

magazines, newspapers, and catalogs

markers

scissors

Click on the *Between the Lions* website!
pbskids.org/lions/gryphonhouse

Song: My House

Games: Monkey Match

Theo's Puzzles (h)

Spider Web

Skill Focus
Creative Expression
Hand-Eye Coordination
Vocabulary

Theme Connections
Animals
Homes and Houses

Vocabulary
crisscross   spider
home   waterspout
legs   web
slit

Materials
black yarn
cardboard squares
markers
paint
pictures of spiders and spider
    webs
plastic spiders
scissors

Preparation
- Provide an 8-inch cardboard square for each child. Cut 1-inch slits around the outside edges of the square.

What to Do

✳ Sing this familiar song about spiders together, having the children add motions.

The Itsy-Bitsy Spider
The itsy-bitsy spider
Climbed up the waterspout.
Down came the rain
And washed the spider out.
Up came the sun
And dried out all the rain.
And the itsy-bitsy spider
Climbed up the spout again.

✳ Show the children pictures of spiders and spider webs. Tell them that many spiders make their homes in webs.
✳ Have the children make spider webs by wrapping black yarn back and forth from one slit to another as they crisscross a cardboard square.
✳ The children may want to put plastic spiders on their webs.

Extension Idea
The children can make fingerprint spiders by pressing a finger into paint, pressing it onto paper, and then drawing eight legs on the fingerprint to make a spider.

Skill Focus

Comprehension
Creative Expression
Fine Motor Skills
Positional Words

Theme Connections

Animals
Homes and Houses

3-D Houses

AGE 4+

Preparation

- Cut a door into each cardboard box. Cut only three sides of the door so it can open and close.

What to Do

* Tell the children that they will make cardboard houses for the pigs in "The Three Little Pigs."
* Talk about the materials that each pig used to build his house.
* Have the children glue dried grass or straw onto the first box, twigs onto the second box, and red paper rectangles onto the third box.
* Point out the parts of the house as the children work: *door, floor, window,* and *roof.* Have the children glue a tiny box onto the roof of the brick house to make a chimney.

Extension Idea

The children may wish to use the houses in the Block, Library, or Pretend and Play Centers. As they set up the houses, ask questions that encourage the children to use positional words. *Where should I put the second little pig's house? Let's put the stick house* next to *the straw house. Which house has a chimney* on top*? Where does the house with the chimney belong?*

Vocabulary

between	next to
brick	on top
chimney	roof
door	second
first	straw
floor	third
in front of	twig
materials	window

Materials

crayons
dried grass or straw
glue
red paper rectangles
scissors
small cardboard boxes
small twigs or sticks

Click on the *Between the Lions* website!
pbskids.org/lions/gryphonhouse

Stories: Beeper Paints
The Three Little Pigs

AGE 3+

Don't Fence Me In!

Skill Focus
Hand-Eye Coordination
Patterns
Vocabulary

Theme Connections
Colors
Homes and Houses
Opposites (Tall and Short)

Vocabulary

around	metal
brick	pattern
concrete	stones
fence	wall
mesh	wood

Materials
building blocks
cardboard box
pictures of fences and brick
    walls

What to Do

❋ Many homes have fences around them. The fences might be made of wood, concrete, stones, bricks, metal and mesh, or other materials.

❋ Place a cardboard box to use for a house in the Block Center. Invite the children to build a fence all the way around the house.

❋ Suggest that they use the blocks to create a fence that has a pattern, such as red block, blue block, red block, blue block or tall block, tall block, short block, tall block, tall block, short block.

❋ Encourage the children to use their creativity as they build their fences.

Extension Idea

Older children may enjoy building brick walls around the house. Show pictures of red brick walls. Look at the way the bricks are stacked one on top of the other. To keep the wall from falling over, the second row of bricks is stacked so that half of each brick is over one brick and half is over the next brick. Suggest that the children build a wall using this stacking pattern.

Skill Focus

Cause and Effect

Hand-Eye Coordination

Vocabulary

Theme Connection

Homes and Houses

Opposites (Yes and No)

BLOCK CENTER

Build a Sturdy House

AGE 4+

Preparation

- Make a two-column chart. Title the chart "Will my house fall down in a wind storm?" Label the columns Yes and No.

What to Do

※ Invite the children to use different materials to build a house that they think will be sturdy.

※ Ask, *What do you think will happen if a storm comes and the winds start to blow really hard? Will your house fall down?*

※ Have the children record their guesses on the chart. Model this process by building a house with cards and then thinking aloud, *I don't think my house of cards is very sturdy. I am going to put my name card under the word* yes *on the chart.*

※ Have the children pretend to be a storm and blow on the card house to see what happens.

※ The children can choose a building material, build their own houses, and then determine whether their house will fall down in a storm.

※ The children pretend to be a storm and blow on the houses they built.

※ Ask the children which house they would prefer to live in and why. Ask, *Which houses are sturdy? Which house you like to live in, and why?*

Vocabulary

build	storm
construct	structure
fall	sturdy
house	wind

Materials

building blocks

cardboard boxes

chart paper

drinking straws

index cards

Legos

markers

modeling clay

nonfiction books about houses
    and construction (See page
    223 for suggestions.)

playing cards

thin pieces of cardboard

Click on the Between the Lions website!
pbskids.org/lions/gryphonhouse

Video Clip: Cliff Hanger Sells His House

Game: Opposite Bunny: built/demolished, sad/happy

LIBRARY CENTER

The Three Little Pigs

Skill Focus
Book Appreciation
Book Care and Handling
Compare and Contrast
Concepts of Print

Theme Connections
Animals
Homes and Houses

Vocabulary

author   same
different   three
folktale   version
illustrator   voice
repeat

Materials
audio recorder
different versions of the story "The Three Little Pigs" (For example, by Paul Galdone, Jerry Pinkney, Byron Barton, and others)

Preparation
• Place several versions of "The Three Little Pigs" in the Library Center.

What to Do

✻ Choose a version of "The Three Little Pigs" to read aloud.

✻ After the pattern of the story has been established, invite the children to chime in on the repeated refrains: *I'll huff and I'll puff and I'll blow your house down* and *Not by the hair of my chinny-chin-chin.*

✻ Point to the illustrations to help clarify who is speaking. Encourage the children to create different voices for the wolf and each of the pigs.

✻ Create an audio recording of "The Three Little Pigs" by reading aloud the story and having the children contribute the repeating refrains.

✻ Encourage the children to "read" the book along with the tape. They will love hearing their voices on the tape.

Extension Idea

Invite the children to select other versions of the book and to look at the words and the pictures on their own or with another child. Tell them to look for ways the stories are alike and different.

Click on the Between the Lions website!
pbskids.org/lions/gryphonhouse
Story: The Three Little Pigs

Skill Focus

Book Care and Handling

Choosing Books

Concepts of Print

Theme Connections

Animals

Homes and Houses

Reading Den

AGE 3+

Preparation

- Fill the Library Center with nonfiction books about homes for animals.
- Make a "reading den" by covering a table with a blanket or tablecloth. Make sure three sides are completely covered, leaving an open area at the entrance to the den. Put large pillows inside the den.

What to Do

- Encourage the children to select books about animal homes that interest them.
- Model how to look at the illustrations on a book cover, predict what the book will be about, and decide whether you want to read it. Say, *This book has a picture of a bear and her cub coming out of a den. Yami, you love teddy bears. You might like to read this book to learn about where real bears live.*
- Demonstrate how to hold, handle, and care for a book.
- Show the children where to begin reading and how to turn the pages. Read parts of the book aloud. Pause to discuss the different animals and their homes.
- Use the illustrations in the book to help the children understand the names of different animals, their homes, and the materials they used to build the homes, such as:

  anthill   *beaver lodge*   *bird nest*

  bear den   *beehive*   *crab burrow*

- The children can curl up in the reading den by themselves or with a friend to look at the words and the pictures in the books they've chosen.

Vocabulary

ant	crab
anthill	den
author	handle
bear	hive
beaver	illustration
bee	lodge
bird	nest
burrow	predict
cover	title

Materials

blanket or tablecloth

nonfiction books about animal homes (See page 218 for suggestions.)

table

Click on the *Between the Lions* website!

pbskids.org/lions/gryphonhouse

Stories: Castles, Caves, and Honeycombs

Wonderful Worms

AGE **3+**

1, 2, 3, a Home for Me

Skill Focus

Counting

Rhyming

Vocabulary

Theme Connections

Counting

Homes and Houses

Vocabulary

apartment   high

building   home

container   tall

Materials

plastic people

small boxes without tops

What to Do

* Tell the children that some people live in homes called *apartments*. Explain that there are many apartments in one building, called an *apartment building*. Some apartment buildings are very tall.

* On a table, place small cardboard boxes and a container filled with plastic people. Have the children stack boxes, three high, to make an apartment building. (Stack the boxes so the open side is facing out.)

* Invite the children to play a game called 1, 2, 3, a Home for Me. To play, the children place three people into each apartment. As they count out the people and place them in their new homes, have them chant "1, 2, 3, a Home for Me."

Extension Idea

Say the chant together. Ask the children to name the rhyming words (*three, me*). Play the game again, having the children focus on the number four. Let them make up a chant using the new number, such as "1, 2, 3, 4, this is a home for more."

Click on the *Between the Lions* website!

pbskids.org/lions/gryphonhouse

Song: My House

Skill Focus

Matching

Observe and Describe

Vocabulary

Theme Connections

Animals

Homes and Houses

MATH AND SCIENCE CENTER

Animal Home Match

AGE 4+

Preparation

- Make puzzle pieces. Glue pictures of animals and animal homes on opposite ends of a piece of card stock or sturdy paper to create an animal/animal home card. Cut each card into two puzzle pieces.

What to Do

☒ Sing together the following lively song about animal homes to the tune of "The Farmer in the Dell."

The Bear Lives in the Den
The bear lives in the den
The bear lives in the den
A house for this animal
The bear lives in the den.

Verse 2: The bird lives in the nest.
Verse 3: The snail lives in the shell.
Verse 4: The ant lives in the ground.
Verse 5: The bee lives in the hive.

☒ Tell the children that they are going to play a matching game. In this game, they will match animals and their homes.

☒ Model by thinking aloud as you pick one of the puzzle pieces that has an animal on it: *Here's a snail. Snails live in shells. Here's a shell. Let's put the two cards together!*

☒ As the children make matches, encourage them to talk about the animal and the home with another child.

Vocabulary

animal	hive
ant	home
bear	house
bee	match
bird	nest
cave	pen
fish	pig
ground	pond
habitat	swim

Materials

card stock or sturdy paper
glue
pictures of animals and animal homes

PRETEND AND PLAY CENTER

Piggy Play

Skill Focus

Imaginative Play

Retelling Stories

Sequencing

Theme Connections

Animals

Homes and Houses

Vocabulary

brick	pig
build	retell
first	sequence
house	straw
last	twigs
next	wolf

Materials

glue

pig noses

poster board

scissors

several versions of "The Three Little Pigs" (For example, by Paul Galdone, Jerry Pinkney, Byron Barton, and others.)

Preparation

• Gather the pig noses that the children made in the Art Center activity in the Animals chapter on page 44.

• Use poster board to make a headband for the wolf. Draw and cut out large paper ears. Glue them onto each side of the headband.

What to Do

✳ Invite the children to act out the story of "The Three Little Pigs."

✳ Ask questions to help the children recall the sequence of events in the story, what comes first, next, and last.

✳ The children playing the roles of the three pigs can put on pig noses. Use the wolf headband as a costume for the child playing the role of the wolf.

✳ Encourage the children to use the materials and props as they act out the story.

Extension Idea

On another day, the children may want to act out another story with pigs or a wolf.

Click on the *Between the Lions* website!

pbskids.org/lions/gryphonhouse

Stories: The Three Little Pigs

The Three Little Pigs: A Sequel

Skill Focus

Gross Motor Skills
Observe and Describe
Vocabulary

Theme Connections

Animals
Homes and Houses

Frog and Lily Pads

AGE 3+

What to Do

* Explain that a frog is an amphibian. Amphibians live part of their lives in the water and part on land.
* Frogs have strong hind legs that help them leap long distances. The frog's front legs are short. It uses its front legs to prop itself up when it sits.
* Have the children set out lily pads (green carpet squares) so the frogs can jump across a make-believe pond.
* Challenge the children to jump across the pond to get to the bugs and other insects that the frog intends to eat for dinner. Invite the children to leap like a frog, using their legs to push them forward.

Vocabulary

amphibian	leap
frog	legs
front	lily pad
hind	prop
insect	

Materials

green carpet squares
nonfiction books about frogs and frog habitats (See page 223 for suggestions.)
plastic bugs

Extension Idea

The children may also enjoy playing Leap Frog. In this game, "frogs" are crouched down and lined up in the grassy area where they live. The back frog puts her front legs (hands) on the frog in front of her and leaps over him. She continues leaping over the frogs until she reaches the front of the line. The frog in the back is the next to leap over his friends. Play continues in this way.

Click on the Between the Lions website!
pbskids.org/lions/gryphonhouse

Story: Hide-and-Seek

SAND TABLE CENTER

Build a Castle

Skill Focus

Imaginative Play
Positional Words
Vocabulary

Theme Connections

Homes and Houses
Imagination

Vocabulary

castles	on top of
flag	prince
inside	princess
king	queen
knight	under
next to	

Materials

bucket
Castles, Caves, and Honeycombs
   by Linda Ashman (optional)
cups
fiction and nonfiction books
   about castles, such as *Over
   at the Castle* by Boni
   Ashburn, *Let's Explore a
   Castle* by Nicholas Harris, or
   The Castle of the Cats by
   Eric A. Kimmel
plastic people
plastic sand molds
sand table

Preparation

- Set both fiction and nonfiction books about castles and the people who live in them near the Sand Table.
- Post pictures of real castles on the wall or near the Sand Table.
- Pour enough water into the sand to make it damp but not wet.

What to Do

⁕ Castles are homes for kings, queens, knights, princes, and princesses. Tall towers with flags decorate these enormous homes. Guards surround the castles to protect the people who live in them.
   Note: If possible read *Castles, Caves, and Honeycombs* to the children.

⁕ Have the children work together to build castles fit for a king or queen. They might use their hands to stack and shape the sand. Show them how to use cups, paper towel rolls, buckets, and other objects to mold the sand.

⁕ As the children work, encourage creative thinking, such as adding flags to the tops of towers and wood blocks for drawbridges.

⁕ Ask the children to tell you a story about the people who live in their castle.

Extension Idea

Encourage the children to use positional vocabulary as they play: *What's* on top of *the castle? Who is that* in front of *the castle?*

Click on the *Between the Lions* website!
pbskids.org/lions/gryphonhouse

Story: Castles, Caves, and Honeycombs

Skill Focus
Concepts of Print

Early Writing

Theme Connections
All About Me

Families

Homes and Houses

WRITING CENTER

I Live Here

AGE 4+

Preparation
• Provide a page for each child. Write this sentence on each page: _____ lives here.

What to Do

✳ Tell the children that you are going to create a book called "Our Homes." Each child will contribute a page to the book.

✳ Brainstorm kinds of homes that boys and girls live in, such as a *house, an apartment, a mobile home, a boat*, and a *condominium.*

✳ Have the children draw pictures of the inside or the outside of their home.

✳ Read the sentence frame together: "_____ lives here."

✳ Point out the beginning and end of each word and the spaces between the words.

✳ Have the children fill in their names.

✳ Ask the children questions to encourage them to talk about their picture. *What color is your house (condo, trailer)? What is your favorite room?* Write their responses in a sentence or caption under their drawing.

✳ Point to each word as you read the words with the child.

✳ Compile the pages into a class book. Create a cover.

Vocabulary

apartment	house
boat	mobile home
book	room
condominium	sentence
cover	spaces
create	words
home	write

Materials
crayons

heavy paper

markers

scissors

stapler

Click on the *Between the Lions* website!
pbskids.org/lions/gryphonhouse

Story: Beeper Paints

Song: My House

WRITING CENTER

AGE 4+

A Bird's Home

Skill Focus
Concepts of Print
Early Writing (Print Conveys
　Meaning)

Theme Connections
Animals
Homes and Houses

Vocabulary

bird	nest
cotton	stick
grass	straw
moss	string
mud	twig

Materials

bird nest or mud and straw,
　grass, twigs, sticks, moss,
　cotton, and/or string
crayons
magnifying glass
pencils
picture of a bird nest
writing paper

Preparation

- If you do not have a real bird nest, shape one from mud and straw, grass, twigs, sticks, moss, cotton, and/or string. Let it dry before putting it into the learning center.
- Make a word card for *nest*. Write the word and glue a picture of a nest on the card.

What to Do

* Talk about nests and what kinds of animals build nests. Ask, *What do you think a bird might use to make a nest?*
* Have the children examine a bird's nest with a magnifying glass.
* Ask the children to write the word *nest* on their paper. Then encourage them to draw or write about each item they see in the nest.
* As the children share their lists, ask, *Where do you think the birds got the twigs or moss? What will the bird do with the finished nest?*

Extension Idea

Help the children write the names of the items. You might say, Moss *begins with the same letter as your name, Maggie. What letter is that? Write the letter "Mm" by the picture you drew of the moss.*

Click on the *Between the Lions* website!
pbskids.org/lions/gryphonhouse

Story: Castles, Caves, and Honeycombs
Video Clips: If You Were: eagle
　　　　　　Cliff Hanger and the Nightingales

CHAPTER 10

Music

Strike up the band! It's time to make instruments, explore the sounds created by each, and have a concert. The children will learn about the world of music as they experiment with loud and soft sounds, high and low sounds, and fast and slow music. The fun and learning continue when the children dance to the music.

I Am a Fine Musician

I am a fine musician,
I practice every day.
And people come from miles around,
Just to hear me play
My tuba, my tuba.
I love to play my tuba.
Oom-pa oom-pa, oom-pa oom-pa,
* oom-pa oom-pa, oom!*

AGE 4+

Musical Letters

Skill Focus
Compare and Contrast
Letter Recognition
Vocabulary

Theme Connections
The Alphabet
Music

Vocabulary
big	lowercase
curvy	match
find	straight line
letter	uppercase
little	

Materials
blank index cards
box
cookie sheet
glue or tape
magnetic letters
markers
pictures of musical instruments
   from magazines or catalogs

Preparation
- Use blank index cards and markers to make a card for each musical instrument. On the card, write the first letter of the name of each instrument in both uppercase and lowercase letters and the full name of the musical instrument. Glue a picture of the instrument on the card.
- Place all the magnetic letters into a box.

What to Do

✴ Display the letter/musical instrument cards. Explain that each card has an uppercase and lowercase letter that is the first letter of the name of the musical instrument pictured on the card.

✴ Say, *This cards shows an uppercase (big) "M," a lowercase (little) "m" and a picture of maracas. In this box, there are some letters. We're going to find all the first letters of the names of musical instruments and put them on the cookie sheet.*

✴ Have the children sort the letters. As they take the letters out of the box, comment on their shapes. Say, *This letter has two straight lines and two slanted lines, just like the big "M" on the "maracas" card. It's an "M!" Let's put it here on it the cookie sheet. This letter has curvy lines. It does not match the letters on any of the musical instrument cards, so we are not going to put it on the cookie sheet.*

✴ Have the children sort the remaining letters. When they've finished, encourage them to identify the letters and the musical instruments.

Click on the *Between the Lions* website!
pbskids.org/lions/gryphonhouse

Story: The Ants and the Grasshopper
Song: Upper and Lowercase
Games: Monkey Match

Skill Focus

Fine Motor Skills
Letter Recognition
Name Recognition

Theme Connections

The Alphabet
Music

ABC CENTER
Name Collages

AGE
4+

Preparation

- Cut out multiple letters of the alphabet from old magazines, advertisements, and greeting cards. The letters should be large and colorful.
- As an example, write *Cleo* on an index card. Cut out and glue or tape of picture of Cleo on the card.

What to Do

✳ Display the name card with Cleo's name and her picture. Explain that Cleo, one of the characters on *Between the Lions*, loves to sing and dance to music. Show the children how to make a name collage by selecting the letters in Cleo's name and pasting them in order onto a piece of construction paper.

✳ Can the children guess what is Cleo's favorite color? Using a marker in the suggested color, write *Cleo* under the cutout letters on the collage.

✳ Invite the children to select the letters in their own names and make their own name collages.

✳ Post the collages on a bulletin board.

Vocabulary

alphabet   match
collage   name
letter   word

Materials

construction paper
crayons
cutout letters from old
    magazines, advertisements,
    and greeting cards
glue sticks
index cards
markers
picture of Cleo, one of the
    characters on *Between the
    Lions* (Use a search engine to
    find a photograph of Cleo.)

Cleo

Click on the *Between the Lions* website!
pbskids.org/lions/gryphonhouse

Song: Upper and Lowercase

ART CENTER

Make a Horn

Skill Focus
Creative Expression
Experimenting with Sound
Listening

Theme Connections
Music
Shapes
Sounds

Vocabulary

bay	quiet
blow	saxophone
fast	slow
horn	soft
hum	toot
loud	trumpet
music	wail

Materials

art scraps (beads, bits of ribbon, buttons, wallpaper, fabric, feathers, sequins, sparkles, aluminum foil, yarn)
cardboard paper towel rolls
glue
rubber bands
scissors
wax paper

Preparation
• Cut wax paper circles about twice the size of the opening at the end of the cardboard tubes. You will need one tube per child.

What to Do

✳ Have the children use the cardboard tubes and other materials to make and decorate horns (kazoos).

✳ Encourage them to cover their horns with foil, wallpaper, or fabric. They might also wish to glue interesting materials on their horns, such as sequins, sparkles, buttons, and feathers.

✳ Help the children wrap a piece of wax paper over one end of their horn and secure it with a rubber band.

✳ Help the children write their names on their horns.

✳ Invite the children to practice humming into and tooting their horns—loudly, then quietly. Encourage them to play fast and slow songs.

Extension Idea

Let the children experiment making sounds with their horns. Can they make them wail like saxophones? Or bay like trumpets? How many different sounds can they produce?

Click on the *Between the Lions* website!
pbskids.org/lions/gryphonhouse

Story: What Instrument Does Alvin Play?
Poem: Tuning Up
Video Clip: Fred Says: kazoo

Skill Focus

Creative Expression

Fine Motor Skills

Listening

Theme Connections

Colors

Feelings

Music

Musical Murals

AGE 3+

Preparation

- Hang mural paper across a wall at the children's height. Use a pencil to mark boundaries for each child's artwork.
- Set out shallow trays of blue paint. Make tints and shades of blue by mixing in different amounts of white or black paint.
- You may wish to clip clothespin "handles" onto the crumpled rags so the children don't touch the paint with their hands.

What to Do

⁕ Play blues music from *Even Kids Get the Blues* or other recordings. Tell the children that the blues is a special kind of music that is sometimes played with different kinds of horns. The songs are usually sad.

⁕ Encourage the children to paint to the music using only blue paint. Demonstrate how to dip a rag into the paint and paint with it.

⁕ Help each child write his name under the section of the painting that he created.

⁕ Look at the mural together, inviting the children to describe how the music and the paintings make them feel.

Extension Idea

Place books in the Art Center about music, jazz, and the blues. Invite the children to draw or paint instruments that are played in jazz and blues bands.

Vocabulary

blues	sad
jazz	saxophone
music	trombone
paint	trumpet
rags	

Materials

CD player

cloth rags (about 3" x 3")

clothespins

Even Kids Get the Blues CD by the Re-Bops or another CD

masking tape

mural paper

paint (blue, white, black)

shallow foam trays

Click on the *Between the Lions* website!

pbskids.org/lions/gryphonhouse

Story: Yesterday I Had the Blues

Video Clip: Cliff Hanger Sings the Blues

ART CENTER

Tambourines, Rattles, and Maracas

Skill Focus
Creative Expression
Fine Motor Skills
Listening to Sounds
Vocabulary

Theme Connections
Music | Sounds
Opposites (Fast and Slow)

Vocabulary
back	rhythm
front	shake
instrument	slap
pour	tambourine
rattle	tap

Materials
colorful paper
feathers
glue
heavy paper plates
masking tape
paint
paintbrushes
pieces of fabric
ribbon
small plastic bottles with tops
small rattling objects (bells, small beads, buttons, paper clips, or small pebbles)
yarn

What to Do
❉ Tap, tap, tap and rattle, rattle, rattle with these great homemade rythm instruments.

Tambourines
▫ Have the children use art materials to decorate the backs of two heavy paper plates.
▫ Tape the two plates together with the insides facing each other. Leave a section open so the children can pour in a handful of small beads, buttons, or small bells, then finish taping the edges.

Maracas or Rattles
▫ Let each child fill a plastic bottle with small rattling objects, such as paper clips, buttons, or pebbles.Screw the lids on tightly.
▫ Encourage them to decorate their instruments by tying feathers, ribbons, yarn, or pieces of fabric around the necks of the bottles.
▫ Ask the children to write their name onto masking tape and attach the labels to the bottom of their instruments.
▫ Engage the children in exploring different ways to play their instruments. They can shake them, tap them, and slap them against their legs.

Extension Ideas
❉ Clap different rhythms, both fast and slow, and have the children play them back with their instruments.

Click on the *Between the Lions* website!
pbskids.org/lions/gryphonhouse

Story: Violet's Music
Poem: Tuning Up
Game: Dub Cubs

Skill Focus

Creative Expression

Exploring Sound and Rhythm

Listening

Phonological Awareness
   (Syllables)

Theme Connections

Music | Sounds

Brush and Tap

AGE 3+

What to Do

✳ Brush, brush, brush and rap, tap, tap, using these instruments made from wooden blocks.

Rhythm Sticks

▫ Let the children experiment with long, cylinder blocks. Model how to tap two "rhythm sticks" together to create a beat.

▫ Encourage the children to say familiar rhymes as they tap to the rhythm of the words.

Jack and Jill

Jack and Jill went up the hill
To fetch a pail of water.
Jack fell down and broke his crown
And Jill came tumbling after.

Sandpaper Blocks

▫ As the children play in the Block Center, invite them to make sandpaper block instruments.

▫ Show them how to wrap a strip of sandpaper around a wooden block and secure the sandpaper with masking tape.

▫ To play sandpaper blocks, have the children rub them together. The result is a soft brushing sound. The children can tap blocks together for a louder sound.

▫ Play music with a strong beat. Have the children rub or tap the sandpaper blocks in time to the music.

Vocabulary

beat	rhythm sticks
brush	sandpaper
cylinder	blocks
instrument	tap
rhythm	

Materials

CD player

CD with children's music

masking tape

sandpaper strips

wooden blocks

Click on the Between the Lions website!

pbskids.org/lions/gryphonhouse

Video Clip: Fred: Musical Instruments

Game: Dub Cubs

LIBRARY CENTER

Rattlesnake Song

Skill Focus

Book Appreciation

Comprehension

Vocabulary

Theme Connections

Animals

Music

Sounds

Vocabulary

cactus	prairie dog
council	rabbit
crushing	rattlesnake
darted out	saguaro
desert	scattered
excited	sobs
foolish	trail
illustrations	turtle
lizard	whirled
maiden	

Materials

Baby Rattlesnake by Lynn
    Moroney

magnifying glass

maracas

rattle

What to Do

✳ Read aloud *Baby Rattlesnake*.

✳ Invite the children to chime in on the Baby Rattlesnake's song—
"Ch-Ch-Ch! Ch-Ch-Ch!"

✳ Point to the illustrations of the desert landscape to clarify the
meaning of unfamiliar words, such as *cactus, saguaro, rabbit,
turtle,* and *prairie dog.*

✳ Use words and gestures to explain the meaning of words and
phrases such as *whirled, excited, sob, darted out, neat in her dress,*
and *trail.*

✳ Invite the children to look at the book again on their own or
with another child.

✳ Encourage them to retell the events as they look at the pages.
Set rattles and maracas in the learning center, and invite the
children to use them to enhance the sound of Baby Rattlesnake's
eerie song.

Extension Idea

Suggest that the children look at the illustrations with a
magnifying glass. See what details they can find on the skins of the
lizard and snake.

Click on the *Between the Lions* website!
pbskids.org/lions/gryphonhouse

Song: We Choose to Cha Cha Cha
Video Clip: Choppers Chop, Shoppers Shop

Skill Focus

Book Awareness

Phonological Awareness
  (Rhythm and Repetition)

Theme Connections

All About Me

Music

Read, Read, Read a Book

AGE **4+**

Preparation

• Fill the Library Center with fiction and nonfiction books about music and musical instruments.

What to Do

✳ Sing this song to the tune of "Row, Row, Row Your Boat."

Read, Read, Read a Book
Read, read, read a book
Every single day,
Merrily, merrily, merrily, merrily
Every single day.

✳ Add motions to the song by opening your hands and pretending to hold and read a book.

✳ Ask the children to sing along with you.

✳ Invite them to sing the song as they select books that interest them from the browsing boxes.

✳ Encourage them to look at the words and pictures on their own or with another child.

✳ Model how to look at the illustration on a book cover, predict what the book will be about, and decide whether you want to read it. Go over basic library rules and how to handle and care for books.

Vocabulary

book   picture
cover   read
illustration rules
instrument   title
music

Materials

fiction and nonfiction books
   about music and musical
   instruments (See page 224
   for suggestions.)

Click on the Between the Lions website!
pbskids.org/lions/gryphonhouse

Stories: Violet's Music
         What Instrument Does Alvin Play?
Song: Read a Book Today!

MATH AND SCIENCE CENTER

Sound Shakers

AGE 3+

Skill Focus
Compare and Contrast
Listening
Matching Sounds
Vocabulary

Theme Connections
Music | Sound

Vocabulary
different	same
matching	shake
pair	sound

Materials
12 identical containers with lids
   (such as yogurt containers)
glue
small objects (such as beads,
   buttons, coins, marbles,
   pebbles, paper clips, sand)

Preparation
* To make sound shakers, fill containers with small objects so you have six matching pairs of shakers—two with coins, two with sand, and so on.
* Glue the lids into place.

What to Do
* Tell the children that in this center they will play a game in which they try to find sounds that are the same.
* Set out the sound shakers. Encourage the children to gently shake one container, listening to the sound of the objects inside. Tell them to find the matching sound by shaking the remaining containers.
* When the children find the matching sound, set the pair of sound shakers aside.
* Continue until all of the sound shakers are matched.

Extension Idea
Add new pairs of sound shakers to the Math and Science Center. As the children match the containers, encourage them to describe the sound made by the objects inside.

Click on the *Between the Lions* website!
pbskids.org/lions/gryphonhouse
Song: Very Loud, Very Big, Very Metal
Video Clips: Opposite Bunny: loud/quiet
   The Trampolini Brothers: noisy, noisier, noisiest

Skill Focus

Cause and Effect
Compare and Contrast
Experiment with Sounds
Vocabulary

Theme Connections

Music | Sounds
Opposites (Thick and Thin, High and Low)

Rubber Band Guitars

AGE
3+

What to Do

❋ Have the children make homemade guitars by first decorating the boxes.

❋ Help the children write their names on the boxes.

❋ Help them count out three rubber bands. The rubber bands should be three different widths.

❋ Compare the rubber bands. Ask, *Which is thickest? Which is thinnest?* Have the children stretch the rubber bands around the box, placing them in order from thickest to thinnest.

❋ Show the young guitarists how to pluck the strings on their guitar.

❋ Listen closely to the sound made by each rubber band. Say, *This rubber band makes the lowest (deepest) sound. I can see that it is the thickest rubber band. Which rubber band makes the highest sound?*

❋ Encourage the children to explore making different sounds on their rubber band guitars.

Extension Idea

Let the children try a different arrangement of rubber bands. Does the box guitar sound different? Let the children engage in free play, playing their guitars as they sing their favorite songs.

Vocabulary

guitar	string
higher	thickest
lower	thinnest
pluck	vibrate
sound	

Materials

crayons
empty tissue boxes (or other small boxes that are open on one side)
markers
rubber bands (in three different widths)

Click on the *Between the Lions* website!
pbskids.org/lions/gryphonhouse

Story: Violet's Music
Game: Dub Cubs

PRETEND AND PLAY CENTER

AGE 4+

Join the Band

Skill Focus
Creative Expression
Imaginative Play
Listening to Music
Movement

Theme Connections
All About Me
Instruments | Music

Vocabulary
audience   musicians
band   singer
microphone
musical
   instruments

Materials
CD or tape player
CDs or tapes of children's songs
   (See page 227 for
   suggestions.)
musical instruments (child-
   made or toy)
play microphone or paper towel
   tube and aluminum foil
scarves (for dancing or dress
   up)
Violet's Music by Angela
   Johnson

Preparation
- If you don't have a toy microphone, make one by wrapping a paper towel roll in aluminum foil.

What to Do
- ✳ Read aloud the book *Violet's Music*.
- ✳ Tell the children that Violet always wanted to play guitar. One day while strumming her guitar in the park, she meets other children who play instruments. They form a band so they can play music together.
- ✳ Invite the children to form a band, playing instruments they have made.
- ✳ Encourage the children to name and talk about the different musical instruments in their band.
- ✳ What will they call their band? Have them draw or write a banner with the name of their band on it.
- ✳ Play recordings of children's songs. Invite the band to play along with the music.

Extension Idea
Have a performance, letting the band play for the group. Other children may wish to sing or dance to the music or be the audience.

Click on the *Between the Lions* website!
pbskids.org/lions/gryphonhouse

Stories: Violet's Music
                What Instrument Does Alvin Play?
Poem: Tuning Up

Skill Focus

Creative Expression

Listening and Speaking

Recall and Retell

Vocabulary

Theme Connections

Animals

Music | Sounds

PRETEND AND PLAY CENTER

Baby Rattlesnake

What to Do

* Share the book *Baby Rattlesnake* with the children.
* Turn the pages and look at the pictures together to review the events in the story. Talk about what happens in the beginning of the story, the middle, and the end.
* Engage the children in dramatic play and storytelling as they act out the beginning of the story.
* The children can decide who will play the roles of Baby Rattlesnake, Mother, and Father.
* Let them dress up and use props appropriate for their characters. For example, Father Rattlesnake may want to put on a hat and Baby Rattlesnake needs a rattle (or tambourine).
* As the children act out the story, prompt Baby Rattlesnake to cry "Waah-h-h! I want a rattle." After Mother and Father give him a rattle, encourage Baby Rattlesnake to play his or her rattle.
* Everyone can join in as they make up and sing a rattlesnake song.

Extension Idea

Interested children may make up a rattlesnake dance and teach it to the class.

Vocabulary

beginning	rattle
cry	rattlesnake
end	smash
middle	tambourine

Materials

Baby Rattlesnake by Lynn
   Moroney

props (hats, scarves, maracas or
   rattles)

SAND TABLE CENTER

Musical Letter Molds

Skill Focus
Fine Motor Skills

Letter Recognition

Theme Connections
The Alphabet

Music

Vocabulary

curvy	mold
first	sand
letter	straight
line	trace
lowercase	uppercase

Materials

glue or tape

index cards

markers

pictures of a horn, tambourine,
   and maracas from
      magazines or catalogs

plastic letter molds

sand

sand table

scissors

Preparation

- Write the uppercase and lowercase "Hh," "Tt," and "Mm" on index cards to create letter cards for "Hh," "Tt," and "Mm."
- Draw or cut out and glue a picture of a horn, tambourine, and maracas on index cards. Write the word for each picture to create word cards.

What to Do

✳ Select one letter of the alphabet. Focus on a letter that relates to music and musical instruments. In this case, the letter "Hh" is the example.

✳ Display the letter "Hh" card, and trace over the straight lines and then the curvy line to show how the letters are formed.

✳ Encourage the children to write uppercase "H" and lowercase "h" in the sand. Then have the children press molds for the letters "H" and "h" into the sand to make raised letters. Have them trace the letters with their fingers.

✳ Say, *You made the letter "h"! It's the first letter in the word* horn. Have the children point out the "h" on the word card *horn*.

✳ Add to the center new letter cards "Tt" and "Mm" and word cards for *tambourine* and *maracas*.

Extension Idea

Help the children use letter molds to make the word *horn* in the sand. Provide the word card for them to match letters.

Click on the *Between the Lions* website!
pbskids.org/lions/gryphonhouse

Game: Monkey Match

Skill Focus

Early Writing

Letter Recognition

Shapes

Theme Connections

Music

Shapes

Sounds

Triangles

AGE **4+**

Preparation

- Cut out 8-inch paper triangles. Punch a hole into the top of each and put a loop of string through the hole.

What to Do

◼ Let the children hold up the triangle (musical instrument) by the string and tap the inside or the outside.

◼ Talk about the three sides that form the shape of the triangle—one straight line on the bottom and two straight lines, slanted to meet at the top.

◼ Have the children run their fingers around the paper triangles to feel the shape.

◼ Ask each child to draw pictures of triangles and objects that are shaped like triangles.

◼ Encourage them to label the objects. Perhaps they can write the beginning letter of the word. Model, by saying, *I drew a tent. It has three sides like the triangle.* Tent *begins with the /t/ sound. The letter "T" stands for that sound. I am going to write the letter "T" by my tent.*

Vocabulary

letter   straight line

mobile   triangle

slanted line   write

Materials

clothes hanger

crayons

hole punch

pencils

yarn

tagboard or other stiff paper

triangle (musical instrument)

yarn

Extension Idea

Make a Triangle Mobile. String yarn through the hole in the top of each paper triangle. Have the children help to tie the triangles to a coat hanger and hang the coat hanger from the ceiling.

Click on the *Between the Lions* website!

pbskids.org/lions/gryphonhouse

Story: What Instrument Does Alvin Play?

Video Clip: Shapes

I Love It!

Skill Focus
Concepts of Print
Creative Expression
Early Writing

Theme Connections
All About Me
Music

Vocabulary

caption   side by side
display   trace
name   words
read   write
sentence

Materials

drawing paper
markers and/or crayons
pencils
tape

Preparation

• Write the sentence frame *I love to* _____ on each child's paper.

What to Do

✳ Think about characters you've read about that like music. For example, say, *Violet loves to play the guitar. Baby Rattlesnake loves to shake her rattle.*

✳ Have each child draw a picture of something he loves to do when he hears music.

✳ Ask each child to write his name on his page.

✳ Encourage each of them to write a word to complete the sentence: I love to _____. The children may scribble, write letter-like symbols, letters, or words.

✳ Tape all of the pages together, side by side, and display on the wall for the class to "read" together.

✳ As each child shares his own work, write the word he uses to complete the sentence. Have him trace over the word.

Extension Idea

The children may want to dictate additional sentences about their pictures. Write each child's words. Think aloud as you write, pointing out the beginning and ending of each word and the spaces between words.

Click on the *Between the Lions* website!
pbskids.org/lions/gryphonhouse

Story: Violet's Music
Game: Dub Cubs

CHAPTER 11

Nighttime

Things that make noises in the dark of the night can cause powerful emotions and stir up fears. However, in this chapter, the children explore the amazing sights, sounds, and smells of the night. Favorite nighttime lullabies, bedtime stories, and rituals comfort children. Searching for stars in the sky and hunting for animal tracks spark curiosity and provide opportunities for reading, writing, and sharing ideas.

Reach for the Stars

Bend and reach, reach for the stars.
Here comes Jupiter, there goes Mars.
Bend and stretch, reach for the sky,
Stand on tiptoes, oh, so high.

ABC CENTER

Silvery, Shiny "Ss"

Skill Focus
Creative Expression
Fine Motor Skills
Letter Recognition

Theme Connections
The Alphabet
Nighttime

Vocabulary
diamond
letter
lowercase
silver
sky

star
sticker
twinkle
uppercase
wonder

Materials
aluminum foil
construction paper
glue
index card
marker
scissors
star stickers

Preparation
• Write the word *stars* on an index card.
• Draw and cut very large outlines of uppercase "S" and a lowercase "s" from construction paper. Make enough for each child to have one of each.
• Cut aluminum foil in 1-, 2-, and 3-inch squares.

What to Do

✳ Sing the song "Twinkle, Twinkle, Little Star" with the children.

Twinkle, Twinkle, Little Star
Twinkle, twinkle, little star. (*Open and close fingers.*)
How I wonder what you are! (*Tap head with finger.*)
Up above the world so high. (*Reach up to the sky.*)
Like a diamond in the sky. (*Make a diamond shape with hands.*)
Twinkle, twinkle, little star. (*Open and close fingers.*)
How I wonder what you are! (*Tap head with finger.*)

✳ Hold up the *stars* word card and read it. Ask, *What is the first letter in the word* stars? *What is the last letter?*
✳ Provide a large uppercase "S" and a lowercase "s" for each child. Invite them to decorate the letters with pieces of foil and star stickers.
✳ Invite the children to describe the silvery letter "Ss" that sparkles with stars.

Click on the *Between the Lions* website!
pbskids.org/lions/gryphonhouse
Story: A Shower of Stars
Song: Without an s
Game: Theo's Puzzles(s)

Skill Focus

Letter Recognition
Vocabulary
Word Recognition

Theme Connections

The Alphabet
Nighttime

Search for s-t-a-r

AGE 4+

Preparation

- Place a large box in the ABC Center. Set the box on its side so the opening faces the children.
- Place star, moon, and planet stickers on the inside walls of the box.
- Scatter plastic letters inside the box.
- Drape fabric over the opening so the box is dark.
- Write the word *star* on an index card.

What to Do

✳ Display the *star* word card.

✳ Have the children read the word with you and identify the first letter: "s."

✳ Suggest that the children use a flashlight to search through the night-sky box for the letters in *star*, then arrange the letters to match the letters on the word card.

Extension Idea

Repeat the activity using word cards for *sky*, *planet*, and *moon*.

Vocabulary

moon
night
planet

sky
star

Materials

dark scarf or fabric
index card
large box
lowercase plastic letters that include the letters "s," "t," "a," and "r"
marker
small flashlight
stickers (stars, moon, planets)
word cards for *star*, *sky*, *moon*, *planets*

Click on the *Between the Lions* website!
pbskids.org/lions/gryphonhouse

Story: A Shower of Stars
Song: Mighty Star Lion
Game: Sky Riding

ART CENTER

Star Paintings

Skill Focus
Creative Expression
Fine Motor Skills
Shape Recognition

Theme Connections
Nighttime
Shapes

Vocabulary
glitter	slanted
painting	sparkly
shape	sprinkle
shine	star
sides	tilt

Materials
black construction paper
large box lids
large glitter
glue
glue tray
newspaper
star-shaped cookie cutters
writing materials, including a
   white marker

Preparation
• Place box lids in the Art Center. Encourage the children to put their papers into a lid as they work.
• Cover the tables in the Art Center with newspaper.

What to Do

✳ Look at star-shaped cookie cutters. Have the children run their fingers around the outside to feel the shape of the star. Point out that a star has many slanted lines and five points. Count them.

✳ Invite the children to make star paintings on black construction paper.

✳ Show the children how to dip the star cookie cutter into glue and press it onto the black paper.

✳ Sprinkle the sparkly glitter over the glue on the paper, and then tilt the paper to cover the entire glued area.

✳ Gently shake off the excess glitter.

✳ Encourage creativity as the children complete their star paintings.

✳ Remind the children to clean up the center to prepare it for the next group of children.

Extension Idea

Explain to the children that artists usually sign their artwork. Help them use a white marker to write their name on the black paper and to give their painting a title.

Click on the *Between the Lions* website!
pbskids.org/lions/gryphonhouse
Song: Mighty Star Lion

Skill Focus
Creative Expression
Fine Motor Skills
Vocabulary

Theme Connections
Animals
Colors
Nighttime

Night Scenes

AGE 3+

Preparation
• Cover the tables in the Art Center with newspaper.

What to Do

✳ Encourage the children to look at the illustrations in *Night in the Country*. Talk about the animals that come out at night and the colors in the night scenes.

✳ Have the children draw a nighttime scene. Suggest that they press down hard on the crayon while drawing. Tell them *not* to color the sky.

✳ When the drawings are complete, have the children brush the entire picture with black paint.

✳ Have them lay the paintings on a flat surface. Watch for the night scene to appear as the paint dries!

Extension Idea

Ask the children to describe their night scenes. Ask, *What color is the sky? What other colors can you see? What animals are in your night scene? What is your favorite part of the painting?*

Vocabulary
deer	owl
house	rabbit
moon	raccoon
night	sky
nighttime	stars

Materials
container of watered-down
   black paint
crayons
newspaper
Night in the Country by Cynthia
   Rylant
paper
smocks
wide paintbrushes

Click on the *Between the Lions* website!
pbskids.org/lions/gryphonhouse

Story: Night in the Country

Night on the Mountain

AGE 4+

Skill Focus
Hand-Eye Coordination
Imaginative Play
Vocabulary

Theme Connections
Animals
Nighttime
Shapes

Vocabulary
clearing   polar bear
icy   shape
mountain   sky
night   snow

Materials
blocks
blue paper
construction paper
pencil
pictures of bears and mountains
    from *Polar Bear Night* or your
    own picture collections
scissors
star and moon stencils (or
    cookie cutters)
toy animals

Preparation
- Trace star and moon shapes onto construction paper. Cut out as many as desired.
- Decorate the Block Center with the star and moon shapes against a background of blue paper.

What to Do
✳ Show the children illustrations of bears and mountains from *Polar Bear Night* or your own picture collections.
✳ Explain that many polar bears live where the weather is icy and cold and the mountains are tall.
✳ Talk about the shapes of the mountains, including the jagged edges and the different levels.
✳ Invite the children to build snow mountains with blocks.
✳ Set out toy bears and other animals and encourage the children to have them climb the mountains and look at the night sky.

Extension Idea
Encourage the children to build other block scenes where the animals can look at the stars. Maybe the scenes are the top of a tree or barn or a clearing in the woods.

Click on the *Between the Lions* website!
pbskids.org/lions/gryphonhouse
Story: Night in the Country

Skill Focus
Gross Motor Skills

Hand-Eye Coordination

Rhyming

Theme Connections
Animals

Nighttime

Shapes

"Hey, Diddle, Diddle"

AGE 4+

What to Do

❋ Recite this familiar nursery rhyme, pausing to have the children supply the rhyming words *fiddle* (rhyming with *diddle*) and *spoon* (rhyming with *moon*).

Hey Diddle Diddle
Hey, diddle diddle, the cat and the fiddle,
The cow jumped over the moon.
The little dog laughed to see such sport,
And the dish ran away with the spoon!

❋ Invite the children to build the outline of the moon with blocks.

❋ The children can say the rhyme in unison as they play the role of the cow and jump over the moon.

Extension Idea

Describe the different shapes of the moon (crescent moon, half moon, full moon), and invite the children to build each.

Vocabulary

crescent moon   moon

fiddle   rhyme

full moon   sport

half moon

Materials

blocks

LIBRARY CENTER

AGE **3+**

Bedtime Stories

Skill Focus
Book Appreciation
Choosing a Book

Theme Connection
Nighttime

Vocabulary

author	nighttime
bedtime	pictures
cover	read
fiction	select
illustrations	sleep

Materials

books about bedtime (See page 218 for suggestions.)
box
markers
paper
scissors
tape or glue

Preparation

• Set out a browsing box with books about bedtime.

What to Do

▣ Teach the children this song about books. Sing to the tune of "Lazy Mary."

This Is the Way We Hold Our Books
This is the way we hold our books,
Hold our books, hold our books.
This is the way we hold our books
When we are busy reading.

Verse 2: This is the way we open our books….
Verse 3: This is the way we turn a page….

▣ Set out the browsing box and encourage the children to select books about bedtime that interest them and to look at the words and illustrations on their own or with a friend.
▣ Invite the children to draw a picture of their favorite things in the books.

Click on the *Between the Lions* website!
pbskids.org/lions/gryphonhouse
Song: Read a Book Today!

Skill Focus

Book Appreciation

Phonological Awareness
(Repeated Sounds)

Theme Connections

All About Me

Nighttime

Lullaby Stories

AGE
3+

Preparation

- Fill the Library Center with the children's favorite lullaby stories.
- Add a nightlight and big pillows.

What to Do

🔅 Remind the children that the Library Center has many different kinds of books. The books are kept in browsing boxes to help the children find books about a specific theme.

🔅 Sing this variation on a traditional song.

A-Hunting We Will Go
A-hunting we will go!
A-hunting we will go!
We'll find ourselves a favorite book,
And then to bed we'll go.

🔅 Talk to the children about bedtime. Ask, *Do you like to listen to a story at bedtime? Does someone ever sing you a lullaby? What do you do to help yourself fall asleep?*

🔅 Ask the children to find their favorite lullaby books.

🔅 Invite them to curl up on the pillows in the Library Center to look at the illustrations and "read" the story on their own or with another child.

Extension Idea

Have the children make a book cover for their favorite story. They can use alphabet stamps to write the title and then color a picture to show what the book is about.

Vocabulary

bedtime	hunt
books	hunting
classroom	library
favorite	lullaby
find	

Materials

alphabet stamps

big pillows

crayons

drawing paper

nightlight

traditional lullabies (See page 224 for suggestions.)

Click on the *Between the Lions* website!

pbskids.org/lions/gryphonhouse

Story: Tabby Cat at Night

MATH AND SCIENCE CENTER

Star and Moon Patterns

Skill Focus
Patterns
Shape Recognition
Vocabulary

Theme Connections
Nighttime
Shapes

Vocabulary

circle	planet
extend	points
moon	round
oval	star
pattern	stars

Materials

star and circle shapes (cutout paper, attribute blocks, or plastic shapes)

What to Do

✳ Show the children star and circle shapes. As the children hold the shapes, suggest that they trace the outline of each with their fingers.

✳ Ask them to describe each shape. Say, *The round circle is the moon. This is a star.* Ask, *How many points does the star have?*

✳ Lay the moons and stars in a line on the table to create a pattern: star, star, moon; star, star . . . Touch the shapes as the children name them. Ask, *What shape comes next in this pattern?*

✳ Have the children copy the pattern and add more shapes to continue it, duplicating the pattern.

✳ Invite pairs of children to work together to make new patterns with the shapes.

Extension Idea

On another day, make it more challenging by including color in the pattern. for example: blue star, red star, white moon; blue star, red star....

Click on the *Between the Lions* website!
pbskids.org/lions/gryphonhouse

Story: Worm Is Stuck
Video Clip: Shapes

How Many Stars?

AGE 4+

Skill Focus
Creative Expression
Speaking (Use Language to
    Communicate Ideas)

Theme Connections
Counting
Nighttime

Preparation
- Cut circles from black poster board. Use a hole punch to punch a different number of holes into each circle of poster board. Cut these circles a bit larger than the lens on the flashlight so the children can hold a circle up to the lens of the flashlight without blocking the holes in the circles of poster board.
- Wrap a paper-towel roll in aluminum foil to make a "telescope."
- Tape a black poster board "sky" in the learning center.

Vocabulary
billion	shining
count	sky
flashlight	star
galaxies	telescope
million	trillion
observations	twinkling

Materials
aluminum foil
black construction paper
black poster board
flashlight
hole punch
tape

What to Do

✴ Have the children recite this poem with you.

Can You Count the Stars?
One star, two stars, three stars, four. *(Hold up one, two, three, and four fingers.)*
How many? How many? How many more?
Shining stars up in the sky.
Can you count them? We can try.

✴ Ask, *How many stars are in the sky?* Introduce words for very large numbers, such as *million, billion,* and *trillion.*

✴ One child can place a circle of poster board on top of the lens of her flashlight. As she points it toward the black sky (black paper), tiny "stars" will appear.

✴ Invite another child to look through her telescope to see the stars twinkling on the poster board sky.

✴ Let the children count the stars together.

✴ Switch roles and repeat with other star cards.

Time to Sleep

AGE 3+

Skill Focus
Health Awareness
Listening and Speaking
Vocabulary

Theme Connections
All About Me
Nighttime

Vocabulary

button   routines
lullaby   sleep
nightlight   tie
nighttime   zip
ritual

Materials
blankets
costumes (robes, slippers)
lullaby music
music player
nightlight
rocking chair
sleep mats or cots
stuffed animals

What to Do

✳ Invite the children to talk about their nighttime routine. Ask, *What do you do before you go to sleep at night?* Talk about things that help the children fall asleep (bedtime story, nightlight, special stuffed animal, hug, lullaby, and so on).

✳ Emphasize that everyone needs to sleep. Sleep helps our bodies and minds grow strong. It makes us able to play and learn better, too.

✳ Invite the children to pretend that they are getting ready to go to bed. Let them play soft lullaby music as they engage in dramatic play with nighttime rituals and then going to sleep.

Extension Idea

Add a box of costumes, including robes and sleepers. Let the children practice buttoning, tying, and zipping the costumes as they play.

Click on the *Between the Lions* website!
pbskids.org/lions/gryphonhouse
Story: Tabby Cat at Night
Video Clip: Opposite Bunny: asleep/awake

Skill Focus

Imaginative Play

Listening and Speaking

Vocabulary

Theme Connections

Animals

Nighttime

Sounds

Night Owls

AGE 4+

Preparation

- Cut out pictures of nocturnal animals, and glue them on index cards to make animal picture cards. Label each picture.

What to Do

※ Provide books about animals that look for food and play at night. Explain that they are called nocturnal animals.

※ Use gestures and sound effects to help the children understand the meaning of sounds that animals might make, such as *creak, patter, groan, hoot, howl, thump, squeak*, and *squeal*.

※ Have the children close their eyes and pretend that it is night. Ask, *What sounds can you hear? What animal is making the sound?*

※ Invite the children to play a game of Animal Charades. One child chooses an animal card, makes noises and moves like the animal, and the other children guess the nocturnal animal.

Extension Idea

Have the children draw pictures of other nocturnal animals they have seen.

Vocabulary

creak	noises
frog	owl
groan	patter
hoot	rabbit
howl	raccoon
lick	squeak
night	squeal
nocturnal	thump

Materials

glue

index cards

nonfiction books about nocturnal animals (See pages 224–225 for suggestions.)

pictures of nocturnal animals

Click on the *Between the Lions* website!

pbskids.org/lions/gryphonhouse

Story: Night in the Country

SAND TABLE CENTER

Night Tracks

Skill Focus
Observe and Describe
Speaking and Listening
Use Science Tools

Theme Connections
Animals
Nighttime

Vocabulary

hidden   paw print

lion   rabbit

path   raccoon

paw   track

Materials

corrugated cardboard

glue

magnifying glass

sand

sand table

scissors

thread spools

toy lion, rabbit, raccoon

Preparation

- Draw pawprints on corrugated cardboard. Cut out the pawprints. Glue a thread spool onto the back of each one for a handle.
- Pour just enough water into the sand table to make the sand damp.

What to Do

✳ Ask the children if they have ever seen a paw print. Say, *You can find out where the animal is hiding or where it has been by following the tracks.*

✳ Show the cardboard paw prints and identify which animal made each.

✳ Model how to make rabbit tracks in the sand. Press the cardboard paw firmly into the sand. Continue, making a path across the sand table. At the other end, dig a hole and hide a toy rabbit.

✳ Have the children follow the tracks to the rabbit hole.

✳ Invite the children to make new tracks in the sand that lead to each hidden animal.

Extension Idea

Encourage the children to use a magnifying glass to get a closer look at the paw prints.

Click on the *Between the Lions* website!
pbskids.org/lions/gryphonhouse

Story: Rabbit's Gift

Skill Focus
Concepts of Print
Listening and Speaking
Writing Name

Theme Connections
All About Me
Feelings
Nighttime | Shapes

Wish Upon a Star

AGE 4+

Preparation
- Cut out large paper stars, one for each child.
- Use a hole punch to punch a hole in the top of each star.

What to Do

※ Invite the children to close their eyes and imagine seeing a star in the night sky.

※ Say a wishing-on-a-star rhyme together. Explain that a wish is something you hope will come true.

Star Light, Star Bright
Star light, star bright,
First star I see tonight.
I wish I may,
I wish I might
Have the wish
I wish tonight.

※ Ask the children to think of a wish. Help them come up with ideas. Ask questions such as, *What do you wish you could play outside? What do you wish we could have for snack?*

※ Let the children write their name on one side of a paper star.

※ On the other side, encourage them to draw a picture of their wish and to write about it. They may use scribbles, symbols, letters, or words.

※ Help the children hang the stars from a clothes hanger to make a Wish Upon a Star Mobile.

Vocabulary
come true   secret
hope   star
mobile   wish

Materials
clothes hanger
crayons
hole punch
large cutout star shapes
pencils
yarn

Click on the *Between the Lions* website!
pbskids.org/lions/gryphonhouse

Video Clip: Cliff Hanger and the Wish Upon a Star

WRITING CENTER

Picture Dictionary

Skill Focus
Letter Recognition
Letter-Sound Correspondence
Phonological Awareness
 (Beginning Sounds)

Theme Connections
Alphabet
Nighttime | Sounds

Vocabulary

begin	nocturnal
dictionary	picture
first letter	sound
night	word

Materials

crayons
drawing paper
nonfiction books about
 nocturnal animals (See
 pages 224–225 for
 suggestions.)
pencils
simple picture dictionary

What to Do

* Show the children a very simple picture dictionary.
* Turn the pages, noting that the pages have a letter of the alphabet written on them. Look for "Aa," "Bb," and "Cc."
* Show the "Bb" page. Say the names of the pictures. Help the children realize that all of the words on that page begin with the letter "Bb" and have the /b/ sound.
* Create a Picture Dictionary of Night Animals. Have the children create pages for the picture dictionary.
* Invite them to write a letter at the top of their page. Then draw one or more pictures of animals that come out at night on the page. The animal names should begin with that letter. A few examples include bats, owls, cats, foxes, mice, raccoons, skunks, opossums, and fireflies.

Extension Idea

Assemble a class book with the children. Leave it in the Library Center for the children to read on their own or with others. Encourage them to add additional pages as they learn about new nocturnal animals.

Click on the *Between the Lions* website!
pbskids.org/lions/gryphonhouse
Story: Night in the Country
Games: Monkey Match (Beginning Sounds)
 Theo's Puzzles

Plants

With this topic, the children in your classroom take a look at plants and how they grow. After looking at books about a variety of plants, the children get down and dirty, digging up seeds, planting beans, and exploring flowers. The children will explore butterflies, engaging in dramatic play and writing activities to learn about those amazing winged insects that have a life-long connection to plants.

Dig the Earth
(Tune: "Row, Row, Row Your Boat")

Dig, dig, dig the earth (make digging motion)
Then we plant our seeds. (pretend to drop seeds)
A gentle rain, (flutter fingers down)
And bright sunshine (circle arms
  above head)
Are what our flowers need.

ABC CENTER

Letter Shaping "Ss"

Skill Focus
Fine Motor Skills
Letter Formation
Letter Recognition

Theme Connections
The Alphabet
Plants
Shapes

Vocabulary
clay
curvy line
find
hunt
lowercase

roll
search
seed
trace
uppercase

Materials
blank small and large
   index cards
marker
modeling clay
pipe cleaners
seeds

Preparation
• Write the uppercase and lowercase "Ss" on one large index card and several small index cards to create "Ss" letter cards.

What to Do
✳ Select one letter of the alphabet. Focus on a letter that relates to a topic of interest to the children, a book you are reading to the children, or something that is happening in the classroom related to plants. In this case, the letter "Ss" is the example for *seeds*.

✳ Display the large letter "Ss" card. Use your finger to trace over the curvy lines on both the uppercase and lowercase letters to show the children how to form the letter. Point out that the uppercase and lowercase letters look the same, but the lowercase letter is smaller than the uppercase letter.

✳ Have the children glue seeds over the letters on the small letter "Ss" cards to create a tactile letter "Ss" card.

Extension Idea
Show the children how to shape pipe cleaners or to roll "snakes" of clay with the palms of their hands to form the letter "Ss."

Click on the *Between the Lions* website!
pbskids.org/lions/gryphonhouse

Story: Stone Soup
Song: Without an s
Game: Theo's Puzzles (s)

Skill Focus

Fine Motor Skills
Letter Recognition
Vocabulary
Word Recognition

Theme Connections

The Alphabet
Plants

ABC CENTER

Find the "s-e-e-d-s"

AGE 4+

Preparation

- Write *seeds* on an index card to create a word card for seeds. Decorate the card to look like a packet of seeds if desired.
  Note: If you make additional word cards for *potato*, *onion*, and *carrot*, add the appropriate letters to the ABC Center.
- Use the gardening equipment to hide the letters "s," "e," "e," "d," and "s." For example, place an "s" under a package of seeds, an "e" in a flower pot, and a "d" in a gardening glove.

What to Do

✳ Display the *seeds* word card.

✳ Have the children repeat the word with you and identify the first letter: "s."

✳ Suggest that the children find the letters in *seeds*, then arrange the letters to match the letters on the word card.

✳ Remind the children to hide the letters so the ABC Center is ready for the next child or group of children who come to use it.

Extension Idea

Suggest that the children find letters in other words related to plants, such as *potato, onion,* and *carrot.* Tell them to find the letters in order, from the first one in each word to the last one. For example, if the word is *carrot* and they find "r" before "c," they have to put the "r" back until they find the "c", and the "a."

Vocabulary

carrot	match
farmer	onion
first	pot
garden	potato
glove	seeds
last	trowel
letter	word

Materials

blank index cards
gardening equipment, such as
    flower pots, gardening
    gloves (in different sizes and
    colors), trowels, a watering
    can, and seed packages
markers
several sets of plastic letters "s,"
    "e," and "d"

Click on the *Between the Lions* website!
pbskids.org/lions/gryphonhouse

Poem: Little Seeds

ART CENTER

Carrot Garden Mural

AGE 4+

Skill Focus
Creative Expression
Fine Motor Skills
Positional Words
Vocabulary

Theme Connections
Colors
Food | Plants

Vocabulary

above	ground
beet	leaves
below	orange
brown	purple
carrot	root
dirt	soil
green	stem

Materials

carrot, preferably one with the green leaves still attached

glue stick or tape

green crayons, markers, or paint

large sheet of mural paper

large sheets of drawing paper

scissors

small squares of orange construction paper

Preparation

• Hang a sheet of mural paper in the Art Center.
• Draw a horizontal line across the paper. Help the children paint the area below the line brown to represent the "dirt" or "soil".
• Draw the outline of a carrot on large drawing paper. Make one for each child.

What to Do

✳ Show the children a real carrot. Explain that the orange part of a carrot grows under the ground, and the green leaves poke above the ground to get sun. The orange part stays in the dirt to soak up water and nutrients from the ground.

✳ Tell the children that they will be working together to make a carrot mural.

✳ Have the children tear pieces of orange paper and glue them onto the carrot outline.

✳ Invite the children to cut out their carrots and glue or tape them onto the mural. Model how to glue a carrot in the "dirt" area of the paper.

✳ The children can use green markers, crayons, or paint to draw the stems and leaves above the soil line.

Extension Idea

Show the children pictures of beets and explain that they are also roots, and they grow under the ground like carrots. Encourage the children to make purple beets and add them to the mural.

Click on the *Between the Lions* website!
pbskids.org/lions/gryphonhouse

Song: Vegetable Medley
Poem: You Never Hear the Garden Grow
Video Clip: Joy Learno: turnip

Skill Focus

Colors

Creative Expression

Fine Motor Skills

Vocabulary

Theme Connections

Colors

Plants

ART CENTER

Bow Flowers

AGE 4+

Preparation

- Cover the tables with mural paper.
- Pour paint into shallow foam trays. Place one or two bows beside each tray.

What to Do

- ❋ Share colorful picture books about flowers. Look at the illustrations closely and explain that flowers have many petals. The petals are the parts that give the flower its color.
- ❋ Invite the children to make flower prints. Tell them that the flowers will have many bright petals.
- ❋ Have the children dip a bow into a container of paint.
- ❋ Show them how to dab the ribbon gently onto the mural once or twice. Then choose a different bow, dip it into a new color, and dab it onto the paper.
- ❋ As the children create their flower prints, encourage them to fill the mural with flowers of different shapes and colors.
- ❋ The children may want to add stems and leaves with a paintbrush.

Extension Idea

Encourage the children to talk about the parts of the flowers and their shapes and colors. Introduce the words *stem*, *leaves*, *flower*, *petals*, and *bud*.

Vocabulary

blue	mural
bow	petals
bud	print
flower	red
garden	ribbon
green	stem
leaves	yellow

Materials

bows with multiple loops and thick and thin ribbons (at least one for each container of paint)

mural paper

nonfiction books about flowers (See pages 221 for suggestions.)

paint in several colors

paintbrushes

shallow foam trays

smocks

Pop-Up Flowers

AGE 4+

Skill Focus
Creative Expression
Fine Motor Skills
Following Directions
Vocabulary

Theme Connections
Imagination
Plants

Vocabulary
bottom	grow
down	patient
flower	sunshine
ground	up

Materials
art items (big buttons,
    pompoms, yarn)
crayons
foam cups
glue
scissors
white paper
wooden craft sticks

Preparation
• Cut a slit in the bottom of each foam cup.

What to Do

✳ Invite the children to make pop-up flowers. Model the steps.

✳ Help the children color and cut out flower shapes, and then decorate the flowers with pompoms, big buttons, or other art items.
Note: Make sure that each flower is small enough to fit inside the foam cups.

✳ The children can glue the flowers onto one end of their craft sticks.

✳ Hold the cup upright and help each child put the stick down through the middle of the cup and out the slit in the bottom. The flower should be hidden inside the cup.

✳ Have the children sing the song below (to the tune of "I'm a Little Teapot") while they play with their pop-up flowers. Encourage them to make the flower pop out of the cup at the end of the song.

I'm a Little Brown Seed
I'm a little brown seed
In the ground.
I need the sunshine.
I need the rain.
If you are patient,
I will grow.
Out pops a flower!
Grow, grow, grow!

Skill Focus
Hand-Eye Coordination
Imaginative Play
Vocabulary

Theme Connections
Animals
Plants

Worm Tunnels

AGE 4+

What to Do

* Share pictures of worm tunnels. Use illustrations from books such as *Wonderful Worms* by Linda Glaser, *Garden Wigglers* by Nancy Loewen, or others you have read to the children.
* Explain that worms burrow into the soil. The holes and tunnels help water get to the plants.
* Encourage the children to use blocks to build a garden that has a worm tunnel in it. They may want to add block flowers and vegetables to the garden, too.
* Let the children engage in dramatic play by moving the clay or plastic worms through the tunnels.

Vocabulary
burrow   passageways

garden   tunnels

holes   worms

Materials
blocks

nonfiction books about worms
    (See pages 226–227 for
    suggestions.)

paper

pencils

plastic or clay worms

Extension Idea

Provide paper and writing tools. Invite the children to make labels for plants with pictures or words. Have them tape the labels to thin blocks and put them in the garden to show where specific plants are growing.

Click on the *Between the Lions* website!
pbskids.org/lions/gryphonhouse

Story: Wonderful Worms
Video Clip: Fred Says: wiggle

LIBRARY CENTER

Plant Books

Skill Focus
Book Care and Handling
Choosing Books
Concepts of Print

Theme Connections
All About Me
Plants

Vocabulary

author	potato
broccoli	predict
cabbage	pumpkin
care for	rutabaga
cover	seed
eggplant	skin
husk	title
illustration	turnip

Materials

fiction and nonfiction books about plants (See pages 225–226 for suggestions.)

Preparation
• Fill the Library Center with fiction and nonfiction books about plants.

What to Do

✳ Encourage the children to select books that interest them and to look at the words and the pictures on their own or with another child.

✳ Model how to look at the illustrations on a book cover, predict what the book will be about, and decide whether you want to read it. Say, *This book has a picture of an enormous potato on the cover. Look how many people and animals are trying to pull it out of the ground! Who would like to read about a farmer who grows the biggest potato in the world?*

✳ Demonstrate how to hold, handle, and care for a book.

✳ Show the children where to begin reading and how to turn the pages.

✳ Encourage the children to look at the illustrations to help them understand the meaning of unfamiliar words such as: *seed, skin, husk, eggplant, potato, pumpkin, cabbage, rutabaga, broccoli, turnip,* and others.

Extension Idea

Challenge the children to look for story patterns. Some stories, such as *The Enormous Potato,* begin with one character (the farmer). As you go through the book, in each new picture a new person or animal joins in to help solve a problem.

Click on the *Between the Lions* website!
pbskids.org/lions/gryphonhouse

Story: Bump! Thump! Splat!
Song: Read a Book Today!

Skill Focus

Book Appreciation

Compare and Contrast

Making Connections

Theme Connections

Colors

Plants

Illustrators

AGE 4+

What to Do

- ✳ Tell the children that illustrators are artists. Artists have different styles and use different techniques.
- ✳ Display several books by Eric Carle. Turn the pages of one of the books and show how Eric Carle paints designs on papers and then cuts and pastes them to make objects on the page.
- ✳ Encourage the children to select books about plants that interest them and to look at the words and pictures on their own or with another child.
- ✳ Model how to look at the illustrations on a book cover, predict what the book will be about, and decide whether to read it.
- ✳ Invite the children to pay close attention to the illustrations on the pages. Can they pick out books that were illustrated by Eric Carle?

Extension Idea

Set out wallpaper scraps, scissors, and glue. Let the children imitate Eric Carle's unique style and create a picture like one they see in his books.

Vocabulary

artist	illustration
artwork	illustrator
cover	paint
design	predict
illustrate	style

Materials

books illustrated by Eric Carle (See page 227 for suggestions.)

glue

picture books about plants (See pages 225–226 for suggestions.)

scissors

wallpaper scraps

MATH AND SCIENCE CENTER

Compare Carrots

Skill Focus
Compare and Contrast
Measuring
Vocabulary

Theme Connections
The Five Senses
Food
Plants

Vocabulary

compare	order
length	short
long	shorter
longer	shortest
longest	

Materials
3–8 fresh carrots in a variety of lengths
masking tape

Preparation
• Place a horizontal line of masking tape on a table in the Math and Science Center.

What to Do

✳ Have the children observe three carrots—touching, smelling, and looking at them. How are they alike, and how they are different?

✳ Let the children compare the lengths of the carrots.

✳ Tell the children to line up the carrots with the tips touching the line of masking tape.

✳ Encourage the children to move the carrots around until they are in order from shortest to longest. Ask, *Which carrot is the shortest? Which is the longest? Show me.*

✳ On another day, add more carrots so that the children are comparing and ordering 4–8 carrots.

Extension Idea

Peel and slice the carrots. Have the children taste a slice from each carrot and determine which one tastes the best. Is it the longest (or the shortest) carrot?

Skill Focus

Compare and Contrast
Observe and Describe
Recognize Plants as Living Things
Vocabulary

Theme Connections

Food
Plants

Bean Sprouts

AGE 3+

Preparation

- Soak beans in water overnight.
- Hang a clothesline across the back of the Math and Science Center. Attach clothespins to the line.

What to Do

* Show the children a handful of lima beans. Explain that a lima bean is a seed. Say, *If we can plant the beans (seeds), lima bean plants will sprout and grow from them.*
* Tell the children they are each going to grow beans.
* Have the children crumple a damp paper towel and place it into a clear bag.
* Ask them to place two beans into the bag. Seal the bag and write their name on it.
* Explain that the beans spent the night in water and that they should be kept damp.
* Have the children hang their bags from the clothesline in the Center.
* Each day, invite the children to look carefully at their beans. Provide a magnifying glass for close inspection.
* The beans will begin to sprout in a few days.

Extension Idea

Invite the children to keep a journal with pictures and notes about the changes happening to the seed. (See My Bean Journal on page 216 for more information.)

Vocabulary

bean   notice
change   seed
damp   sprout

Materials

clear, zip-top sandwich bags
damp paper towels
lima bean seeds, at least two
    for each child
magnifying glass
nonfiction books about seeds
    and plants (See pages
    225–226 for suggestions.)

Click on the *Between the Lions* website!
pbskids.org/lions/gryphonhouse

Poem: You Never Hear the Garden Grow

Flower Shop

AGE 4+

Skill Focus
Environmental Print
Imaginative Play
Listening and Speaking
Sorting

Theme Connections
My Community
Plants

Vocabulary
bouquet
carnation
color words
customer
daisy
florist
flowers
gift card
lily
message
occasion
order
rose
tulip
vase

Materials
artificial flowers
baskets
cans and other containers
class color chart (see Preparation)
markers
nonfiction books about flowers (See page 221 for suggestions.)
paper
pencils
tissue paper
toy cash register
toy telephone

Preparation
• Make a class color chart. Write the names—*red*, *orange*, *yellow*, *green*, *blue*, *purple*, *black*, and *white*—using markers in the corresponding colors.

What to Do
⊠ Talk about flower shops and the jobs people do there.
⊠ Have the children create a play flower store.
⊠ Together, let the children decide on a name for the flower store and create a sign.
⊠ The children can put the artificial flowers into cans or containers and sort them by color. Encourage the children to use the class color chart to help them label the colors.
⊠ Encourage the children to play the roles of a florist and a customer. The florist can arrange flowers, answer the telephone, write flower orders, and write messages for gift cards. The customer may explain who the flowers are for, pick out his favorite flowers, order and pay for them.
⊠ Encourage the children to use names for real flowers, such as *rose, tulip, daisy, carnation,* and *lily.*

Extension Idea
Have the children look at books about flowers and flower shops, such as *Flower Garden* by Eve Bunting and *The Flower Alphabet Book* by Jerry Pallotta, for ideas on how to set up their flower shop and new ways to sort the flowers.

Click on the *Between the Lions* website!
pbskids.org/lions/gryphonhouse

Story: Spicy Hot Colors
Video Clip: Colorful Foods

Skill Focus

Describing Cycles in Nature

Imaginative Play

Recall and Retell

Theme Connections

Animals

Plants

Butterfly Life Cycle

AGE 4+

What to Do

* Read aloud the story *The Very Hungry Caterpillar* by Eric Carle.
* Turn the pages and look at the pictures to help the children recall what happens first (the egg hatches into a caterpillar), next (it eats and eats), then (the caterpillar turns into a chrysalis), and last (it emerges as a butterfly) in the story.
* Encourage the children to engage in dramatic play as they act out the life cycle of a butterfly.
* Invite them to use props such as scarves (wings), antennae headbands, toy fruit, green carpet squares (leaves), and a striped shirt (caterpillar) to enhance the experience.

Vocabulary

big	hungry
butterfly	leaf
caterpillar	little
chrysalis	stomachache
cocoon	wings
egg	

Materials

props (scarves, antennae headbands, toy fruit, green carpet squares, striped shirt)

The Very Hungry Caterpillar by Eric Carle

Extension Idea

For older children, you may want to suggest that one child act as the narrator, while the other children act out the motions.

Click on the *Between the Lions* website!
pbskids.org/lions/gryphonhouse

Poem: Caterpillar

SAND TABLE CENTER

Garden Center

AGE 3+

Skill Focus
Identifying Characteristics of Plants
Using Tools
Vocabulary

Theme Connections
Food
Plants

Vocabulary

almond	orange
apricot	peach
avocado	pit
berry	plum
cherry	rake
lemon	seed
mango	trowel
nectarine	watering can
olive	

Materials
basket
child-sized gardening tools
(rake, trowels, hoe, watering can)
clean soil (optional)
gardening gloves
seeds from lemons, oranges, peaches, avocadoes, plums, nectarines, apricots, cherries, olives, mangoes

Preparation
• Thoroughly wash the seeds and set them in the sun to air dry. When they are dry, put the seeds into a basket.

What to Do

✴ Explore the seeds from different kinds of fruits. Look at some that are small (lemons, oranges, cherries) and some that are quite large (peaches, avocadoes, plums, nectarines, mangoes).

✴ Have the children pretend to plant the large seeds into Theo and Cleo's garden (the sand table).

✴ Invite the children to hoe and rake the surface to loosen the "soil" (the sand)

✴ Show them how to hollow out a spot for a seed using a trowel. Make it deep enough to completely cover the seed.

✴ The children can drop one seed into each hole. Have them cover the hole with sand. Using a watering can, encourage them to sprinkle water onto the newly planted seeds.

✴ Before the children leave the center, they should "harvest" the seeds, pulling them out of the ground and putting them back into the basket for the next group.

Extension Idea

On another day, hide plastic letters in the sand. Have the children dig for the letters. Each time they find a letter, encourage them to name the letter, the sound it stands for, and name of a plant that begins with that letter.

Click on the *Between the Lions* website!
pbskids.org/lions/gryphonhouse
Poem: Little Seeds

Skill Focus

Concepts of Print (Print Conveys
    Meaning)
Dictating Sentences
Fine Motor Skills
Word Recognition

Theme Connections

All About Me | Plants

WRITING CENTER

Hungry Worm Book

AGE 4+

Preparation

- Display picture books about fruits and vegetables.
- Cut a hole into the center of each child's paper. Write this sentence at the bottom of the page: *The worm ate through one _____.*

What to Do

* Explain that the children will be writing pages for a class book called *The Very Hungry Worm Book*. If the children do not know the story, read *The Very Hungry Caterpillar* to them.

* Have the children look at pictures of fruits and vegetables. Ask them to choose one of their favorites.

* Model how to make a page for the class book. Say, *I chose a pineapple for my page. I am going to draw a big pineapple on my paper.* When you finish drawing, say, *Look at the hole in the paper! It looks like the worm has eaten a hole through my pineapple!*

* Read the sentence below the drawing: *The worm ate through one _____.* Ask what word you should write to complete the sentence. As you write, say each letter in the word.

* Invite the children to complete a book page using their favorite fruit or vegetable.

* When all the pages are complete, bind them into a class book and keep it in the writing center.

Vocabulary

ate	fruit
author	hungry
caterpillar	illustrator
eat	sentence
food words	vegetable

Materials

construction paper
crayons
markers
paper
pencils
picture books about fruits and
    vegetables (See page 223
    for suggestions.)
scissors
The Very Hungry Caterpillar by
    Eric Carle, if the children do
    not already know this story

Click on the *Between the Lions* website!
pbskids.org/lions/gryphonhouse

Stories: Otter's Picnic
        Wonderful Worms

WRITING CENTER

My Bean Journal

AGE 4+

Skill Focus
Concepts of Print (Word Spaces)
Dictating Sentences
Observe and Record

Theme Connections
The Alphabet
Plants

Vocabulary

bean	observe
bigger	plant
changes	seed
grow	stem
journal	

Materials
construction paper
crayons
markers
paper
pencils
stapler

Preparation
- Prepare a small journal for each child by folding three sheets of paper in half and placing them inside a piece of construction paper folded in half.
- Staple the book together and number the six pages.
- Write the title *My Bean Book* on the cover.

What to Do
✷ Remind the children that they planted beans in the Math and Science Center (See page 211.)
✷ Give each child a journal.
✷ Explain to the children that they can draw pictures and write notes in the journals about what happens to the bean seeds as they grow.
✷ Read aloud the title of the journal as you point to each word. Point out where you begin and end reading. Talk about the spaces between the words and ask the children to name any letters that they recognize.
✷ Have the children write their names on the covers.
✷ Each day, encourage the children to look closely at the beans. Then, have them draw and write about the changes they notice.
✷ Suggest that they start a new page for each day.

Click on the *Between the Lions* website!
pbskids.org/lions/gryphonhouse
Song: Got a Good Reason to Write
Poem: You Never Hear the Garden Grow

Cleo and Theo's Book Recommendations

Books About Adventures

I Took the Moon for a Walk by Carolyn Curtis
As the sun sets, a young boy takes the moon on a stroll around his neighborhood. Includes information about the phases of the moon and nocturnal animals.

I Want to Be an Astronaut by Byron Barton
A young girl wishes to be an astronaut and thinks about what it would be like to be on a mission into outer space.

Moon Rope (Un lazo a la luna) by Lois Ehlert
Fox wants to go to the moon with his friend Mole, so he comes up with a plan using a rope made of grass in this colorfully illustrated story told in both English and Spanish. [featured on a *Between the Lions* episode]

On My Way to Buy Eggs by Chih-Yuan Chen
When a young Chinese girl is sent to the store to buy eggs, she turns the walk into a wondrous adventure.

On the Go by Ann Morris
Color photographs and simple text show how people around the world move from place to place.

Roller Coaster by Marla Frazee
Roller coasters are big and noisy and scary and… fun! [featured on a *Between the Lions* episode]

Romeo and Lou Blast Off by Derek Anderson
A penguin and polar bear build a pretend rocket ship out of snow and blast off into outer space. Will they ever get home?

Space Boy by Leo Landry
Nicholas packs a snack, puts on his space suit, and takes a rocket to the moon for a quiet picnic.

Tar Beach by Faith Ringgold
Eight-year-old Cassie dreams of flying above her apartment building in Harlem.

Trosclair and the Alligator by Peter Huggins
When Trosclair and his dog head out in a boat to Bee Island Swamp, he figures out a clever way to escape from Gargantua, the giant alligator that lives there. [featured on a *Between the Lions* episode]

We're Going on a Bear Hunt by Michael Rosen
In a variation on this classic chant, a family goes on a bear hunt and they're not scared.

Where the Wild Things Are by Maurice Sendak
When a boy is sent to his room for being too wild, he decides to sail to a land where the real "wild things" are.

Books About The Alphabet

The Alphabet Tree by Leo Lionni
A wordbug teaches the alphabet letters how to become stronger by banding together to form words.

Community Helpers from A–Z by Bobbie Kalman
This alphabet book introduces police officers, firefighters, sanitation workers, veterinarians, and other community workers.

Farm Alphabet Book by Jane Miller
Text and color photographs of a farm accompany each letter of the alphabet.

Jeepers Creepers: A Monstrous ABC by Laura Leuck
Follow a group of little monsters, from A to Z, during a day at school.

Mrs. McTats and Her Houseful of Cats by Alyssa Satin Capucilli
Mrs. McTats starts off with a cat named Abner, but ends up with 24 more and a puppy named Zoom.

What Pete Ate from A to Z by Maira Kalman
Pete the dog eats an accordion and then a variety of outrageous items in alphabetical order.

Books About Animal Homes

Animal Homes by Angela Wilkes
This book introduces the different places and spaces that animals choose to call home.

Barnyard Banter by Denise Fleming
In this rhyming story, all the farm animals are where they should be, except for a missing goose.

Castles, Caves, and Honeycombs by Linda Ashman
Rhyming text and beautiful illustrations introduce the many different kinds of homes where animals live, like a silky web, a sandy dune, and a room inside a warm cocoon. [featured on a *Between the Lions* episode]

Spring Song by Barbara Seuling
Questions and answers invite children to explore what animals do when spring arrives. See also *Winter Song* by the same author.

Whose House? by Barbara Seuling
A boy realizes that each animal has its own perfect place.

The Wonderful House by Margaret Wise Brown
This book tells about many wonderful houses: barns, beehives, bunny holes, and more.

Books About Animals

Animal Babies by Harry McNaught
Simple text and color illustrations describe baby animals and their mothers.

Animals in Winter by Henrietta Bancroft
Simple, factual text and illustrations show what animals do in the winter.

Are You a Snail? by Judy Allen and Tudor Humphries
Witty text and colorful illustrations provide fascinating details about these backyard creatures. [featured on a *Between the Lions* episode]

Brown Bear, Brown Bear, What Do You See? by Bill Martin Jr.
In this classic rhyming book, children see a variety of animals, each one a different color.

Color Farm by Lois Elhert
Colorful cut-out shapes are combined to make pictures of farm animals.

No One Told the Aardvark by Deborah Eaton and Susan Halter
A boy describes all the wonderful things animals get to do, and wonders why he's not allowed to stick out his tongue like an aardvark or eat with his fingers like a chimpanzee. [featured on a *Between the Lions* episode]

Yellow Elephant: A Bright Bestiary by Julie Larios
Rhyming poems describe a variety of colorful animals.

Books About Bedtime

Count the Ways, Little Brown Bear by Jonathan London
Mama Brown Bear assures her cub how much she loves him in this bedtime counting book.

Goodnight Moon by Margaret Wise Brown
In this classic bedtime story, a young rabbit says goodnight to each of the objects in his room.

Grandfather Twilight by Barbara Helen Berger
Grandfather Twilight goes for a walk through the woods as the day draws to a close.

Here Comes the Night by Anne Rockwell
In this soothing story, a mother and son go through their nighttime ritual.

The Night Worker by Kate Banks
A boy goes to work with his father, a construction engineer who works at night.

So Sleepy Story by Uri Shulevitz
A boy is sound asleep until music drifts through his window, causing the boy and everything in his house to dance.

Books About Birthdays

Alicia's Happy Day by Meg Starr
In this bilingual book, everyone greets Alicia as she walks home with her loving extended family.

Birthdays! Celebrating Life Around the World by Eve B. Feldman
Simple text, and paintings by children, show how birthdays are celebrated around the world.

Happy Birthday, Jamela! by Niki Daly
A young South African girl has to get plain shoes for her birthday outfit. When she makes her shoes more festive, a local artist notices.

Henry's First-Moon Birthday by Lenore Look
A young girl helps her grandmother prepare a traditional Chinese celebration to welcome the arrival of her baby brother.

The Secret Birthday Message by Eric Carle
Tim gets a secret, coded message for his birthday. Children can join in as he looks through the clues to find his birthday surprise.

Uno, Dos, Tres: One, Two, Three by Pat Mora
In this rhythmic counting book, two sisters have fun in a Mexican market choosing presents for their mother's birthday.

Books About Clothes

All Kinds of Clothes by Jeri S. Cipriano
This nonfiction book describes the clothing people wear to keep themselves warm or cool.

Hats Hats Hats by Ann Morris
Learn about the many different hats worn around the world.

Joseph Had a Little Overcoat by Simms Taback
A very old overcoat is recycled numerous times into a variety of garments. [featured on a *Between the Lions* episode]

New Clothes for New Year's Day by Hyun-joo Bae
Follow the adventures of a young Korean girl as she prepares for the Lunar New Year.

A New Coat for Anna by Harriet Ziefert
Anna's mother trades the few possessions she has left to get a new coat for Anna.

New Shoes for Sylvia by Johanna Hurwitz
Sylvia gets a pair of beautiful red shoes from her Tia Rosita and finds ways to use them until she grows big enough for them to fit.

Suki's Kimono by Chieri Uegaki
Instead of wearing something new on her first day of school, Suki wears the blue cotton kimono that her grandmother gave her last summer.

Books About Colors

Brown Bear, Brown Bear, What Do You See? by Bill Martin Jr.
In this classic rhyming book, children see a variety of animals, each one a different color.

Chidi Only Likes Blue: An African Book of Colors by Ifeoma Onyefulu
Nneka's little brother only likes blue, until she shows him the beauty of other colors around him.

Colors Everywhere by Tana Hoban
Photographs show the brilliant colors that surround us.

Growing Colors by Bruce McMillan
Photographs of green peas, yellow corn, and other fruits and vegetables show the colors of nature.

My Very First Book of Colors by Eric Carle
This simple book uses nature to introduce colors.

Of Colors and Things by Tana Hoban
This wordless book features photographs of colored objects.

A Rainbow All Around Me by Sandra L. Pinkney
"We are the rainbow—YOU and ME!" declares a multiethnic cast of children who wear, eat, or hold objects of every color.

Spicy Hot Colors: Colores Picantes by
    Sherry Shahan
    Colors explode off the page in this energetic,
    jazzy picture book introducing readers to colors
    in English and Spanish. [featured on a *Between
    the Lions* episode]

Yesterday I Had the Blues by Jeron Ashford Frame
    A young boy uses colors to capture a range of
    emotions, from "down in my shoes blues" to
    the kind of greens that "make you want to be
    Somebody." [featured on a *Between the Lions*
    episode]

Books About Community Workers

Buzz by Janet Wong
    An Asian-American child watches as his
    mommy and daddy get ready for work.
Community Helpers from A–Z by Bobbie Kalman
    This alphabet book for older children
    introduces police officers, firefighters,
    sanitation workers, veterinarians, and other
    community workers.
Everybody Works by Shelly Rotner and
    Ken Kreisler
    Photographs and simple text show how
    everybody works in different ways.

How a House Is Built by Gail Gibbons
    This book describes how the surveyor, heavy
    machinery operators, carpenter crew, plumbers,
    and others work together to build a house.
Teamwork by Ann Morris
    This photo essay shows people from all walks of
    life, all over the world, working together and
    cooperating in teams to get the job done.

Books About Families

Bigmama's by Donald Crews
    The author fondly remembers family visits to
    his grandmother's farm when he was a small
    boy.
Grandfather and I by Helen E. Buckley
    A child tenderly relates how Grandfather is the
    perfect person to spend time with because he is
    never in a hurry. [Also by the same author:
    Grandmother and I.]
I Love You Because You're You by Liza Baker
    In rhyme, a mother describes her love for her
    child no matter what he does.
I Love You Like Crazy Cakes by Rose A. Lewis
    A mother describes going to China to adopt a
    baby girl.
Kevin and His Dad by Irene Smalls
    Kevin has a great time spending a day doing
    chores and playing with his dad. [Also by the
    same author: *My Nana and Me, My Pop Pop
    and Me.*]

My Dog Is as Smelly as Dirty Socks by Hanoch
    Piven
    A little girl describes her family members
    through humorous portraits she's made of them
    using everyday objects. [featured on a *Between
    the Lions* episode]
Quinito's Neighborhood by Ina Cumpiano
    A young boy takes readers on a tour of his
    neighborhood and the people who live there.
    (bilingual English/Spanish text)
The Very Best Daddy of All by Marion Dane Bauer
    Pictures and rhyming text show how some
    fathers—animal, bird, and human—take care of
    their children.
With My Brother/Con Mi Hermano by Eileen Moe
    A young boy enjoys spending time with his
    brother and hopes to be like him when he gets
    older. (bilingual English/Spanish text)

Books About Farms

Cow by Jules Older
This is a light-hearted, informative look at cows—what they eat, how they make milk, and more.

Farmer Brown Shears His Sheep: A Yarn About Wool by Teri Sloat
In this rhyming story, sheep beg to have their wool back, so Farmer Brown knits the yarn into sweaters for them.

Farmer Duck by Martin Waddell
When a hardworking duck nearly collapses from doing a lazy farmer's work, the other animals chase the farmer out of town.

Farming by Gail Gibbons
This book provides an introduction to farming throughout the seasons.

I Love Animals by Flora McDonnell
A girl names all the animals she likes on her farm.

Raising Cows on the Koebel's Farm by Alice K. Flanagan
This book introduces dairy farming with color photographs.

Summer Sun Risin' by W. Nicola-Lisa
A boy marks the passage of the sun as he spends the day on the family farm.

Books About Feelings

The Grouchy Ladybug by Eric Carle
An ill-tempered ladybug goes through the day picking fights with various animals until she realizes that it is better to be pleasant.

The Hello, Goodbye Window by Norton Juster
While visiting her grandparents, a young girl feels happy and sad when she sees her parents coming to pick her up.

Lots of Feelings by Shelley Rotner
Color photographs of children and simple text introduce a range of emotions.

Sam Is Never Scared by Thierry Robberecht
Sam acts as though he isn't scared of anything, though at night he secretly worries that monsters are hiding in his room.

Sometimes I'm Bombaloo by Rachel Vail
Katie is a nice girl, but when her baby brother knocks over the castle she's building, she gets mad… so mad that she becomes Bombaloo!

Today I Feel Silly & Other Moods That Make My Day by Jamie Lee Curtis
Young readers identify and explore their many emotions as they read about a young girl whose mood changes from silly to angry to excited.

Walter Was Worried by Laura Vaccaro Seeger
This alphabet book explores children's emotional reactions to a storm.

When Sophie Gets Angry—Really, Really Angry by Molly Bang
Sophie becomes furious when her mother tells her it's her sister's turn to play with her favorite stuffed gorilla. After some time, Sophie is able to calm herself down.

Yesterday I Had the Blues by Jeron Ashford Frame
A young boy uses colors to capture a range of emotions, from "down in my shoes blues" to the kind of greens that "make you want to be Somebody." [featured on a *Between the Lions* episode]

Books About Flowers

Alison's Zinnia by Anita Lobel
A flower alphabet is brought to life by lushly colored illustrations.

The Flower Alphabet Book by Jerry Pallotta
This alphabet book describes a variety of flowers from A-Z

Planting a Rainbow by Lois Ehlert
A mother and child plant a rainbow of flowers in the family garden.

The Reason for a Flower by Ruth Heller
Rhyming text and bold pictures illustrate pollination and the role of flowers.

What's This? A Seed's Story by Caroline Mockford
A little girl and a bird plant a seed in the spring, wondering what it will be. They watch as the seed grows into a beautiful sunflower.

Books About Food

Bee-bim Bop! by Linda Sue Park
   In playful verse with a bouncy beat, a young girl describes how her mom makes the popular Korean dish called Bee-bim Bop. [featured on a *Between the Lions* episode]

Bread Bread Bread by Ann Morris and Ken Heyman
   Simple text and color photos describe and show the different kinds of bread that people eat around the world.

Bread Is for Eating by David and Phillis Gershator
   A mother sings a song to help her son appreciate the bread that he leaves on his plate. Bilingual text.

Chicks & Salsa by Aaron Reynolds
   The chickens at Nuthatcher Farm get tired of the same old food, so the rooster cooks up a plan for a tasty fiesta. [featured on a *Between the Lions* episode]

Dim Sum for Everyone! by Grace Lin
   While eating dim sum at a Chinese restaurant, family members choose a favorite item from carts brought to their table.

Dumpling Soup by Jama Kim Rattigan
   A Hawaiian family gathers at grandma's house to make dumplings for a New Year's celebration.

Everybody Cooks Rice by Norah Dooley
   A young girl discovers that all of her neighbors, despite their different backgrounds, eat rice. (See also *Everybody Brings Noodles* and *Everybody Bakes Bread* by the same author.)

Jalapeño Bagels by Natasha Wing
   It's International Day at school and Pablo, whose father is Jewish and whose mother is Mexican, must decide what to bring. Includes recipes.

Let's Eat! by Ana Zamorano
   Every day Antonio's mother tries to get everyone to sit down together to eat, but someone is always busy elsewhere.

Stone Soup by Heather Forest
   Two hungry and clever travelers teach a town a lesson in sharing. Includes a soup recipe.

Tortillas and Lullabies/Tortillas y cancioncitas by Lynn Reiser
   Large colorful paintings show three generations sharing family traditions, including making tortillas.

Yum Yum Dim Sum by Amy Wilson Sanger
   Collage illustrations and simple text introduces dim sum to children. [See also *First Book of Sushi,¡Hola! Jalapeño, A Little Bit of Soul Food, Let'sNosh!,* and *Mangia! Mangia!* by the same author.]

Books About Friends

Aggie and Ben: Three Stories by Lori Ries
   In this trio of simple stories, Ben gets a dog that instantly becomes his best friend.

Be Quiet, Marina! by Kirsten DeBear
   Simple text and photographs tell about the friendship between Marina, a noisy girl with cerebral palsy, and Moira, a quiet girl with Down's syndrome.

Bein' with You This Way by W. Nikola-Lisa
   A group of children playing together in the park celebrate their differences. [featured on a *Between the Lions* episode]

Being Friends by Karen Beaumont
   Despite their differences, two girls know that the key to friendship is having one special thing in common: they like being friends.

Best Best Friends by Margaret Chodos-Irvine
   Mary and Clare are best friends, but when Mary gets special attention on her birthday, a jealous Clare is mean to her friend. After a while, they find a way to be friends again.

Earl's Too Cool for Me by Leah Komaiko
   Even though Earl is so cool that he "taught an octopus how to scrub," he is willing to make new friends. [featured on a *Between the Lions* episode]

Lissy's Friends by Grace Lin

Lissy is lonely on her first day of school, so she makes a bird from origami paper to keep her company. Soon she has a group of folded animal friends. When they blow away, a new friend comes to the rescue.

Matthew and Tilly by Rebecca C. Jones

After best friends Matthew and Tilly argue over a broken crayon, they apologize and find a way to be friends again.

My Friend Isabelle by Eliza Woloson

Isabelle and Charlie are friends who like to be together. It doesn't matter that Charlie is tall and fast, while Isabelle, who has Down's syndrome, is short and takes her time.

We Are Best Friends by Aliki

When a boy's best friend moves away, he learns that he can make new friends and still be loyal to his best one.

Yo! Yes? by Chris Raschka

One boy reaches out to another to strike up a new friendship. [featured on a *Between the Lions* episode]

Books About Frogs

A Boy, a Dog, and a Frog by Mercer Mayer

A boy and his dog spot a frog in the water. Can they use a net to catch him? [See also, *A Boy, a Dog, a Frog, and a Friend* and more by this author.]

Hop Jump by Ellen Stoll Walsh

A young frog is tired of the same old hop, jump, hop, so she chooses to dance.

It's Mine! by Leo Lionni

Three selfish frogs argue over who owns their pond and island, until a frightening storm and a wise toad help them see the importance of sharing and cooperation.

Tuesday by David Wiesner

In this wordless story, frogs rise on their lily pads and float through the air.

Books About Fruits and Vegetables

The ABCs of Fruits and Vegetables and Beyond by Steve Charney

This alphabet book includes jokes, tongue twisters, unusual facts, poems, kid-friendly recipes, shopping tips, and more.

Farmers Market by Carmen Parks

A Southwestern family grows and sells fruits and vegetables at the farmers' market.

Growing Colors by Bruce McMillan

Photographs of green peas, yellow corn, and other fruits and vegetables show the colors of nature.

Lunch by Denise Fleming

A mouse nibbles and crunches his way through a meal of brightly colored fruits and vegetables.

The Vegetable Alphabet Book by Jerry Pallotta

Graze through the alphabet in this fun, fact-filled book that begins with asparagus and ends with zucchetta.

We Love Fruit! by Fay Robinson

This book tells about different kinds of fruits and how they grow. (See also *Vegetables, Vegetables* by the same author.)

Books About Houses and Construction

Building a House by Byron Barton

This book describes the steps in building a house.

Homes ABC by Lola Schaefer

This alphabet book features words about houses and homes.

Homes Around the World by Bobbie Kalman

Photographs in this book show the different kinds of houses and homes people live in.

Houses and Homes by Ann Morris

This photographic survey shows houses around the world.

A House Is a House for Me by Mary Ann Hoberman
A rhyming poem describes homes for animals, people, and more.

How a House Is Built by Gail Gibbons
This book describes how the surveyor, heavy machinery operators, carpenter crew, plumbers, and others work together to build a house.

How It Happens at the Building Site by Jenna Anderson
The photographs in this book show a variety of workers building a house.

Wonderful Houses Around the World by Yoshio Komatsu
The photographs in this book show families outside their homes.

Books About Lullabies

All the Pretty Little Horses by Linda Saport
Beautiful pastel illustrations highlight this classic lullaby.

Arrorró, Mi Niño: Latino Lullabies and Gentle Games by Lulu Delacre
A collection of lullabies and fingerplays from various Latin American countries.

Bedtime for Little Bears! by David Bedford
When a polar bear cub refuses to go to sleep, his mother takes him for a walk so he can see how other animals prepare for bed.

Hush, Little Baby by Brian Pinkney
In this version of the classic lullaby, Dad does what he can to soothe his young daughter while Mama does errands.

Sleepy Bears by Mem Fox
Six cubs refuse to settle down until their mother recites a unique rhyming tale that soothes each one.

Time to Sleep by Denise Fleming
Changes in the weather let bear know that it is time for his winter rest. He lets other animals know that it is time to start hibernating.

Where Is Bear? by Leslea Newman
In this rhyming tale, forest animals play hide-and-seek, but Bear can't be found. Where can he be? See also *Skunk's Spring Surprise* by the same author.

Books About Music and Musical Instruments

Ah, Music! by Aliki
A beginner's guide to composers, instruments, artists, and performers, this book includes facts about music history and genres.

Charlie Parker Played Be Bop by Chris Raschka
Shoes, birds, lollipops, and letters dance across the pages to the beat of Charlie Parker's saxophone music. [featured on a *Between the Lions* episode]

The Jazzy Alphabet by Sherry Shahan and Mary Thelan
The letters in this alphabet book boogie.

M Is for Music by Kathleen Krull
This alphabet book introduces musical terms, from anthem to zydeco.

Ms. MacDonald Has a Class by Jan Ormerod
This variation of the "Old MacDonald" song tells about a kindergarten class that visits a farm and creates a performance afterwards.

Music, Music for Everyone by Vera B. Williams
Rosa plays her accordion with her friends in the Oak Street Band and earns money to help her sick grandmother.

My Family Plays Music by Judy Cox
Each member of a girl's family plays a different instrument and enjoys a different type of music—from bluegrass to hymns.

Ruby Sings the Blues by Niki Daly
Everyone teases Ruby because her voice is so loud—until her musician neighbors help her learn to sing and control her volume. [featured on a *Between the Lions* episode]

Violet's Music by Angela Johnson
Violet plays music every chance she gets, and she's always looking for other kids who think and dream music all day long. [featured on a *Between the Lions* episode]

Books About Nocturnal Animals

Daytime and Nighttime Animals by Barbara Behm
Animals are categorized based on the time of day they are active.

One Nighttime Sea by Deborah Lee Rose
Count nighttime animals that live in the sea in this rhythmic counting book.

Owl Moon by Jane Yolen
A girl and her father set out on a cold winter night to find a great horned owl.

The Owl Who Was Afraid of the Dark by Jill Tomlinson
An owlet who is afraid of the dark asks animals and people why they like the dark. Their answers convince him that nighttime is not so scary.

Sleepy Little Owl by Howard Goldsmith
A baby owl plays with his daytime friends, but as he fights to stay awake, he learns that he truly is a night owl.

Snuggle Up, Sleepy Ones by Claire Freedman
As night descends on the jungle, young animals snuggle up to their parents.

Sounds of the Wild: Nighttime by Maurice Pledger
This nonfiction book describes sounds made by night animals in different parts of the world.

A South African Night by Rachel Isadora
Contrasts the activities of people in a city during the day to the activities of the animals at night in a South African nature preserve.

Sweet Dreams: How Animals Sleep by Kimiko Kajikawa
Photos and rhyming text showcase animals at rest.

Books About Outer Space

I Want to Be an Astronaut by Byron Barton
A young girl wishes to be an astronaut and thinks about what it would be like to be on a mission into outer space.

The Moon Book by Gail Gibbons
Lunar phases, eclipses, and a brief history of lunar exploration are described in detail. For older children.

So That's How the Moon Changes Shape by Allan Fowler
This book contains a simple explanation of the moon and why it seems to change shape.

Space Boy by Leo Landry
Nicholas packs a snack, puts on his space suit, and takes a rocket to the moon for a quiet picnic.

Books About Popcorn

Popcorn! by Elaine Landau
This humorous book provides a history of popcorn and will help answer children's questions.

Popcorn Plants by Kathleen V. Kudlinski
This book describes the life cycle of the popcorn plant from the time the farmer plants the seed until the kernel pops.

Books About Restaurants or Grocery Stores

Dim Sum for Everyone! by Grace Lin
While eating dim sum at a Chinese restaurant, family members choose a favorite item from carts brought to their table.

Market Day by Lois Ehlert
Rhyming text and art objects tell of a family's day at a farmers' market.

Books About Seeds and Plants

The Empty Pot by Demi
A young Chinese boy can make anything grow, but he faces a big challenge when the Emperor hands out flower seeds and announces that the child who grows the most beautiful flower will become his successor. [featured on a *Between the Lions* episode]

From Seed to Plant by Gail Gibbons
This simple introduction to plants includes pollination, seed dispersal, and growth from seed to plant.

A Fruit Is a Suitcase for Seeds by Jean Richards
This book illustrates how seeds travel and what they need to grow.

How a Seed Grows by Helene J. Jordan
Children plant bean seeds in eggshells to demonstrate the growth of seeds into plants. [Also available in Spanish].

I'm a Seed by Jean Marzollo
A marigold seed and a mystery seed talk about the changes that take place as they grow. The mystery seed blossoms into a pumpkin.

One Bean by Anne Rockwell
See what happens when a bean is soaked, planted, repotted, and eventually produces a pod with more beans inside.

One Little Seed by Elaine Greenstein
Follow a seed from the time it is planted until it grows into a beautiful sunflower.

The Reason for a Flower by Ruth Heller
Rhyming text and bold pictures illustrate pollination and the role of flowers.

A Seed Grows: My First Look at a Plant's Life Cycle by Pamela Hickman
Children plant and harvest a vegetable garden in their backyard.

Seeds! Seeds! Seeds! by Nancy Elizabeth Wallace
Buddy Bear gets a package from Grandpa that contains five colorful bags of seed activities.

Ten Seeds by Ruth Brown
A counting book featuring seeds and the animals who feast on them.

The Tiny Seed by Eric Carle
Follow the journey of a tiny seed as it faces many obstacles on its way to becoming a flower.

What's This? A Seed's Story by Caroline Mockford
A little girl and a bird plant a seed in the spring, wondering what it will be. They watch as the seed grows into a beautiful sunflower.

Books About Transportation

Flying by Donald Crews
An airplane passes over cities, country areas, lakes, and more. [See also *Freight Train* and *School Bus* by the same author.]

I Love Planes! by Philemon Sturges
A boy dreams about ways of flying and describes his favorite kinds of airplanes. [See also *I Love Trains!* and *I Love Trucks!* by the same author.]

My Car by Byron Barton
Sam describes in loving detail his car and how he drives it. [See also *Planes Board Book*, *Trains Board Book*, and *Boats Board Book* by the same author.]

On the Go by Ann Morris
Color photographs and simple text show how people around the world move from place to place.

This Is the Way We Go to School: A Book About Children Around the World by Edith Baer
Rhyming text and vibrant illustrations describe the many different modes of transportation children all over the world use to get to school.

What Do Wheels Do All Day? by April Jones Prince
Wheels push and spin, race and stroll — wheels help to make us go. [featured on a *Between the Lions* episode]

Books About Worms

Diary of a Worm by Doreen Cronin
> In this humorous story, a young worm discovers that there are some very good and some not so good things about being a worm.

Dirt by Steve Tomecek
> A mole acts as a tour guide in this fact-filled picture book about soil.

Earthworms by Claire Llewellyn and Barrie Watts
> Discover the world of earthworms—how they grow, where they live, what they eat, and who eats them!

An Earthworm's Life by John Himmelman
> This nonfiction book tells about the daily activities and life cycle of the earthworm.

A Handful of Dirt by Raymond Bial
> An eye-opening tour of one of the earth's most precious resources—dirt!

It Could Still Be a Worm by Allan Fowler
> An introduction to earthworms, roundworms, flatworms, and other kinds of worms.

Life in a Bucket of Soil by Alvin Silverstein and Virginia Silverstein
> Learn about the creatures beneath our feet—ants, earthworms, beetles, snails, slugs, and more.

Wiggling Worms at Work by Wendy Pfeffer
> An introduction to earthworms—how they eat, move, reproduce, and help plants grow.

Wonderful Worms by Linda Glaser
> Informative text and illustrations of underground activities reveal how worms help plants grow. [featured on a *Between the Lions* episode]

Books Written by Eric Carle

Draw Me a Star
> An artist's drawing of a star sparks the creation of an entire universe.

The Grouchy Ladybug
> An ill-tempered ladybug goes through the day picking fights with various animals until she realizes that it is better to be pleasant.

The Mixed-Up Chameleon
> A chameleon learns to change his shape as well as his color.

My Very First Book of Colors
> This simple book uses nature to introduce colors.

Papa, Please Get the Moon for Me
> Monica wants the moon to play with, so Papa climbs up a long ladder and waits until it is small enough to carry to bring it to her.

The Secret Birthday Message
> Tim gets a secret, coded message for his birthday. Children can join in as he looks through the clues to find his birthday surprise.

The Tiny Seed
> Follow the journey of a tiny seed as it faces many obstacles on its way to becoming a flower.

Today Is Monday
> Animals eat a different food for each day of the week.

The Very Busy Spider
> A colorful picture book describes a day in the life of a spider.

The Very Clumsy Click Beetle
> A clumsy young click beetle learns to land on its feet.

The Very Lonely Firefly
> A lonely firefly goes out into the night looking for other fireflies.

The Very Quiet Cricket
> A very quiet cricket who wants to rub his wings together and make a sound finally achieves his wish when he meets another cricket.

CDs of Children's Songs

A Child's Celebration of Folk Music by Pete Seeger, Michelle Shocked, Buckwheat Zydeco, Sweet Honey in the Rock, and more

A Child's Celebration of Rock 'n' Roll produced by Music for Little People

Classical Cats: A Children's Introduction to the Orchestra by David Chesky

Ella Jenkins: Multicultural Children's Songs by Ella Jenkins

Even Kids Get the Blues by the Re-Bops

Nicky's Jazz for Kids by Various Artists

The Singable Songs Collection by Raffi

Index of Children's Books

Index